The Girl's Guide to DIY

The Girl's Guide
to DIY

HOW TO FIX THINGS IN YOUR HOME
WITHOUT BREAKING YOUR NAILS

JO BEHARI & ALISON WINFIELD-CHISLETT

First published in 2011 by New Holland Publishers (UK) Ltd
London • Cape Town • Sydney • Auckland

Garfield House
86–88 Edgware Road
London W2 2EA
United Kingdom

Unit 1
66 Gibbes Street
Chatswood, NSW 2067
Australia

80 McKenzie Street
Cape Town 8001
South Africa

218 Lake Road
Northcote, Auckland
New Zealand

ISBN   978 184773 754 0

Publisher: Clare Sayer
Senior Editor: Marilyn Inglis
Designer: Lucy Parissi
Illustrations: Nila Aye at New Division & Stephen Dew
Production: Laurence Poos

1 3 5 7 9 10 8 6 4 2

Reproduction by Modern Age Repro House Ltd, Hong Kong
Printed and bound in India by Replika Press Pvt. Ltd

Note: Unlike our girl on the cover, no sensible DIYer would
ever do DIY in their high heels!

Contents

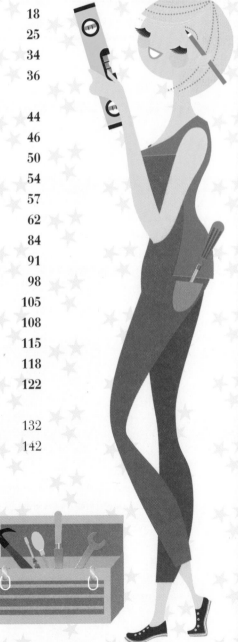

Introduction

You are entering a world of butt joints, stop cocks and rising heads – welcome to *The Girl's Guide to DIY*. If you carry on a little further you might just pick up a skill or two, although you may already possess transferable skills you can use to transform your home. Like following a recipe to produce a fantastic dish, a successful do-it-yourself project is the result of thoughtful planning, putting together the right ingredients, using a method that works, keeping an eye on the clock and adding a splash of flair.

Girls allowed

Despite the title, we hope that everyone can take something from these pages. Even if you are a complete novice, we hope you will be emboldened to give it a go. And don't be daunted by the tools. Think of electric drills as egg beaters on steroids and remember that jigsaws are just sawdust-making cousins of sewing machines. Some beauticians use woodworking files to remove hardened skin from a client's feet during a pedicure! It's the correct tool if it gets the job done.

This book is intended for people with a range of abilities. By learning about tools and how to use them, you can then put these to use with the appropriate materials and techniques that will become skills when practised over time. Plan starter projects in less-frequently used rooms if possible – practice might not make perfect but it will DO.

Remember this is DIY, not master crafts. You'll never produce a dish from a famous chef to the same standard that they will, so don't expect your DIY project to come out like that of a master carpenter. Even if you think you are ham-fisted, can burn hot water and are a menace around the house, we hope you will gain courage and confidence. For those in possession of basic skills already, there are plenty of projects to increase your know-how and we think that even the hardened DIYer will find some tips to add to their repertoire.

Let's talk symbols

Whatever your ability now, this book provides a starting point. We have laid out the projects a bit like a recipe book and hinted at where the task fits in with abilities. So let's talk symbols – each project has been graded with the level of skill and confidence you will need to tackle it: one hammer – easy-peasy; two hammers – a little skill required; while three hammers – makes use of all your talents and skills. You will also see scattered throughout the book a number of TRADE SECRETS and TECHNIQUES boxes (see box below for Symbols explained).

The first part of the book explains the value of good preparation, what to wear and how to get yourself ready to DIY. It also outlines how your home works and what's going on behind your walls. We give you a guided tour around a basic tool kit and tell you how to use them, and there is a pretty comprehensive discussion about materials – what to buy, what to look for. And we also give you an idea of when NOT to do it yourself; sometimes it's just not worth all the hassle and it is better to employ a skilled tradesperson who really knows his or her way around thorny issues

Symbols explained

	EASY-PEASY
	A LITTLE SKILL REQUIRED
	MAKES USE OF ALL YOUR TALENTS AND SKILLS
	TRADE SECRETS
	TECHNIQUES

such as plumbing and electricity. The second part of the book – the projects – includes a whole raft of jobs and projects to try, from hanging stuff on walls to decorating and revamping your kitchen cupboards. We have to admit that most of the projects are biased towards us girls. We show storage solutions for housing your shoe collections, how to hang that fab light shade and how to beautify your home on a budget. To battle against a fear of loud tools, to struggle with new skills and to suffer the thankless task of clearing up afterwards, the goal has to be worth it. For those with an inclination to climb ladders in the rain to clear out and fix gutters, there are other books with that information.

Eco-friendly too!

Where we can we have suggested materials and methods that are kinder to our planet, and kinder to us too. Because not everything can be recycled with no negative environmental impact yet, we have had to stick with more traditional products in some circumstances. We have encouraged the mantra of 'remake, reuse and recycle'. You can feel slightly smug when you breathe new life into an old wardrobe by adding a new shelf, and a tree somewhere will be thanking you for it too!

An argument for brain vs brawn

Not all of us are endowed with big muscles and the stamina of a marathon runner, but being petite isn't a hindrance to successful DIY. There are several ways to compensate for lack of heave ho.

• Let sharp, good-quality tools do the job. Power tools raised the bar and created a lot of equality as far as strength is concerned.

• Use sharp, good-quality drill bits. Let the drill bits work at their maximum ability.

• Replace blades in the jigsaw and sanding paper as soon as these become dull.

• Grip over-tightened nuts with long-handled pliers and use the extra power of the lever effect to aid you. Mechanics use spanner sets because it's the easiest way to loosen something. So should you.

• Use a cordless screwdriver when possible and a long screwdriver if you are using a manual variety. The extra length increases 'torque' and provides more power.

• Loosen screws by spraying WD-40 into the screw. Scratch any hardened paint from the screw slot with a utility knife to maximize the effort.

• When lifting and carrying, carry smaller loads. As long as you get the load moved it doesn't matter how many journeys you make. It's a workout and cheaper than the gym.

• Support heavy stuff by using steps if you have a step ladder or a workbench to hold the other end in place. Use clamps and vices where you can.

Trade secrets

✔ Screws and nails and drill bits need a place to live. A plastic box with separate compartments works well. Keep the different sizes separated so you don't have to sort through every screw to find what you want.

✔ Wall plugs and other small bits of stuff can be kept in a box or a bag to start off with (depending on how much you gather).

✔ Keep old jam jars and jewellery boxes for screws and nails – stick a nail through the top so you know what's in each box before you open it.

✔ If you invest in a tool box, make sure it's big and sturdy enough for you. A tool box isn't just great storage – you can also use it as a mini workbench, you can stand and sit on it if you don't have anything else around.

Wedging and levers

• You can lift heavy things using a lever made from a garden spade or long length of wood. Use a cold chisel or the claw of a hammer to inch under the heavy item and wedge in a long length of wood. Use the other end of the wood as a lever to lift.

• Take breaks. Don't get discouraged by getting exhausted. A nice sit-down with a cup of tea and a biscuit provides a short break to raise blood sugar and plan the next stage.

• HALT – Don't do anything when you are Hungry, Angry, Lonely or Tired. Those strong emotions can help sabotage good work.

• Team up – two ARE stronger than one. Find a friend who has a project in mind and work together on each other's jobs. Setbacks become challenges that you can talk over and putting heads together can turn up a better creative solution.

• Being smaller means you can fit into tighter corners and being nimble often beats brawn in DIY. Holding tiny panel pins is easier if you have smaller hands.

PART I: Before you begin

The door closes. The keys are in your hands. You are finally in your own home. Maybe elation is arising or despair is descending. It can be overwhelming to look at a new home and know where to begin. Perhaps every room needs something changing but you have to move in regardless. You may hate every colour the previous occupant used. If money is tight, there may seem to be no budget to renovate. Whatever the reason, the desire to do everything may clash with a lack of confidence and the result is that nothing gets done. Once all your furniture is in place it can be easy to rationalize that it's too late now, or to allow apathy to gain the upper hand. However, there is always something you can DIY to cheer things up.

ONE STEP AT A TIME

Brace yourself. You CAN do it. Choose small bits of work. However much that pattern offends, deciding to remove ALL the wallpaper from every room at the same time will invariably leave you exhausted and demotivated. Instead tackle one wall at a time. Set a goal to change one thing about one room every week.

There are several really easy quick fixes that will brighten up your home and help change that depressing space into a happy land. Even if your place is a dingy rental property, changing simple things that can be replaced at the end of the lease will make it seem more like a home. Have a look at the projects section for easy fixes to brighten up your mood and make you feel safe and secure.

GSI (GET SOMEONE IN) vs DIY

Some jobs are simply not suitable for the DIY treatment, either because they are too complex and have safety issues, or because you just don't have time. So if you are going to Get Someone In (GSI as opposed to DIY), here are a few things you need to know before you do.

The best way to get someone who is reliable and trustworthy is to ask people you know for recommendations. Make sure you get a number of estimates. The bigger the job, the more estimates you should get. For something like a bathroom refit, three is a good number but for something more complex like a loft conversion or extension then perhaps five. When a tradesperson

visits, they should be respectful of your home and listen to what you want. And remember your gut instinct is a very powerful tool; if you don't get a good feeling about someone then don't use them.

An estimate should come through promptly, showing that the person is serious about the work. It should be very detailed and outline all the work that needs doing and include notes that need to be considered when the work is being undertaken, i.e. if there might be potential additional work once the job starts.

Getting a quote

People often confuse estimates and quotes. It is a common belief that a quote is a fixed price for the job and an estimate is a rough idea of what it might cost. It is often confusing and it is difficult to separate the two in law, so it is important to clarify with the tradesperson the detail of work they will be doing and, if any additional work is necessary, that you are consulted and the cost agreed beforehand.

A good tradesperson will outline each stage of the work and the costs associated. Materials and labour costs should be separated out and if there is likely to be any additional work, a note should be attached to the estimate or quote so you are aware beforehand. This is not always possible as unforeseen problems do arise when work is in progress. If the unforeseen does arise, make sure you see the problems that have occurred, make the effort to see it while the tradesperson is there so they can show you and discuss the solutions.

Don't be afraid to ask questions no matter how

dumb they might seem. This is your home and you have the right to understand the work that is taking place. If you are paying for an estimate then you should be getting a more consultative approach. It is not uncommon, especially in larger jobs, for a tradesperson to provide a less detailed estimate initially and then when you have decided to choose them, they may visit again and spend more time talking through the finer details.

Supporting material

An estimate should be supported by additional materials such as testimonials, copies of insurances and details of terms and conditions. If they don't provide this kind of information, don't be afraid to ask for it. If you are having a very large job done then try to speak to the previous client directly and if you can, go and see the work yourself. If you build up a friendly relationship with a tradesperson, don't be afraid to ask their advice for projects you want to tackle on your own. Most will be flattered enough to share their knowledge. Even if you feel a

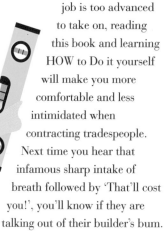

job is too advanced to take on, reading this book and learning HOW to Do it yourself will make you more comfortable and less intimidated when contracting tradespeople. Next time you hear that infamous sharp intake of breath followed by 'That'll cost you!', you'll know if they are talking out of their builder's bum.

PREPARATION

We are all familiar with cookery programmes where the calm chef surrounds him or herself with a multitude of tiny glass bowls of ingredients in expectation of a smooth performance. You will find that like the TV chef, your project will run much more smoothly if you have taken time to lay out all the tools and materials before starting.

Un DIYing

Each generation morphs their homes to reflect their individuality and times. In the 1950s when DIY became all the rage, everyone was busy boxing in the banisters and covering panel doors to simulate 'modern' flush doors. Now we are ripping out what went before. More than likely as you become more confident, you will want to take out something old and replace it. Check out the Tool kit section to learn how to hold a cold chisel and claw hammer to remove old work (see page 32).

Scheduling time

Obviously don't plan a project just before a big wedding, going away on holiday or an important work deadline. Although DIY can become a delightful distraction, it can also drag you down if you are drowning in a project when you should be prioritizing something else. Although toddlers can happily live around bags of dusty plaster, you might find your spirits flagging trying to keep up appearances day in and day out.

Where to work

Consider your work place. You don't need an enormous garage packed with state-of-the-art machinery or even a humble shed at the bottom of the garden; they are luxuries that aren't required to get a DIY job done well. The most practical area in many homes is the kitchen. It is likely to have a work surface that won't wobble and a floor that is easy to clean. The disadvantage is that mealtimes may interrupt grand preparations. You can use kitchen chairs as a simple trestle for cutting wood. Remember to cover them with a drop cloth. If

 Trade secret

Place your mobile phone in a clear plastic sandwich bag before you begin. This extra piece of preparation will be worthwhile if you receive a phone call while your fingers are covered in wood filler or bath sealant.

using the work surface, protect it with newspaper or cardboard. A portable bench vice will clamp onto a counter or table – protect these with a fold of cardboard. A hallway can be commandeered for a project and stairs make useful work trestles.

Get started

Early. Leave yourself enough time to hunt out the tools and discover any extra items you will need to buy. This includes an inspection of any half-used filler or sealant that may have hardened over time. There is potential for exasperation if you arrive at the hardware shop after it has closed.

What tools will you need? Like a recipe, you will need to gather your equipment and tools in the work area. Use a bucket to carry tools and have a small cardboard box (a shoe box is ideal!) in whch to place small items; that way they won't get kicked into can't-find-it land.

If the work you are doing is messy, think about dust sheets, spare clothes and rags to wipe down and clean hands. If you gather these first it will save valuable mopping-up time if something spills.

Trade secret

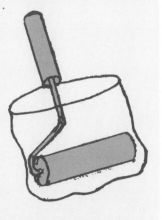

Wrap your paint brushes and rollers in clingfilm or a plastic bag to stop them drying out overnight. If you wash them through they may not be dry enough to use the next day so this works a treat. You can also leave them in the freezer overnight but remember to keep these away from food.

Clearing up

As with preparation at the beginning, it's also important to leave plenty of time to clear up. It's really tempting once you've finished a job to want to show off your success to friends but just remember that leaving time for clear up makes the next job go faster. When you are carrying on a project the following day, make sure you have cleaned any gunk (paint, filler, glue) from your tools and leave them somewhere to dry so that they can be used again quickly.

To **clean brushes** properly, use water and washing-up liquid for soluble paints and white spirit for oil-based paints. Run a filling knife down a roller to get the excess paint off and keep the water running. For oil-based paints, leave brushes to soak in white spirit for 30 minutes or so then run through with warm water and washing-up liquid to clean thoroughly. Dry bushes flat to stop water running into the handle and loosening the bristle adhesive.

Don't be tempted to leave your brushes standing in paint cleaner for days. The bristles will bend out of shape. If you don't clean your brushes properly, they will go crusty and won't be very effective when used again and you'll have to buy new brushes.

Clean your filling knives or spatulas quickly, otherwise filler dries on the blade and the bumps make it impossible to get a smooth flat surface when you come back to use them. It's useful to have a narrow spatula and one with a wider blade and when you clean them, you can use one knife against the other to scrape off excess the excess gunk. But be careful because the edges of these knives are very sharp and can cause nasty cuts.

Put all your tools away in the right place. No one likes it when something goes missing. Shake your drop cloths outside and away from the wind otherwise when you next come to use them, they could be the wrong way up and you will have the last project's dust and debris all over your floor before you even start.

 ## Quick tips

Don't forget to clean yourself. Clean paint off your skin using olive oil if nothing else works and check all over for stray flecks and splodges. It can be quite embarrassing to go out on a Saturday night and have someone kindly point out that you have a big fleck of paint on your back.

What not to wear . . .

Many physical activities require specialist clothing. Although you don't need the latest technological ski jacket en piste, most of us would not set off downhill in an evening dress. So it is with DIY. Taking a few moments to make sure you are dressed appropriately will help avoid injury and prevent ruining your favourite pair of jeans. Once dressed for the job you will feel more confident.

✔ Remove dangly jewellery and bangles. They can get caught up in tools and drag into paint.

✔ Tie back your long flowing tresses.

✔ Choose a work outfit. It might be old jeans and T-shirt, leggings and sweater, shorts and crop top, but whatever the look, let it be something that can stand up to a little paint and a bit of sawdust.

✔ Loose clothing gets caught, billows on to new paint and isn't a good thing. Bear in mind that a

knitted jumper will hold sawdust much more than woven items.

✔ Choose flat well-fitting shoes with toes – trainers are ideal. Tripping isn't funny and dropping a heavy hammer on your bare toes is really not a good look.

DIY accessories

The classic DIY apron has a bib front and wraps around the side. It ends below your knees and has a generous pocket to hold extra screws and small tools when you are working up a ladder. You can wipe your hands on it and keep the rest of your clothing fairly clean.

Make sure you wear **eye goggles** when drilling or sawing wood. Hunting for a tiny speck of sawdust in your eye takes a lot

of time and is painful. A pair of **gardening gloves** instills confidence when picking up rough timber and handling drill bits and the drill. The best are

made of breathable cloth with latex-dipped fingertips for maximum sensitivity combined with protection. Many people fuss over protecting their hands but for a lot of jobs, the extra dexterity and agility of bare hands is best. Use a good gardening barrier cream before a job and clean up with baby oil and then gentle soap to prevent chapped hands at the end of the day. Plan your next manicure for after your big project is done.

Buy a set of **dust masks** and wear them when sanding or using a jigsaw. A classic bandana will protect and hold back your hair for that retro look. It

will prevent you getting paint splashes and sawdust in your hair, giving you that 'premature hint of grey' look. Consider wearing a shower cap for really dusty work or painting ceilings if no one is around. Not glam but it works!

Invest in some knee pads if you are about to begin any flooring job, laying vinyl tiles or caulking up draughty holes. Most available pads are very large and can chafe, but you can make your own by wrapping thermal socks around your knees. A garden kneeling mat can work just as well, although it's not attached to you so you'll have to keep moving it along the job as you progress.

A SHORT GUIDE TO HOUSE CONSTRUCTION

WALL CONSTRUCTION

Depending on the type of property you are in, your home is likely to have the following types of interior walls. Most modern buildings and flats will have a majority of plasterboard (stud walls) but older properties will have stronger walls.

The walls between two internal rooms can be either stud walls (see below) or solid walls. Solid walls are usually supporting walls – supporting the weight of the walls above. To remove these walls involves major structural work and it is not a job for a DIYer; if you want to investigate whether you can do this, you will need to get a builder in and possibly take advice from a surveyor or structural engineer. If your wall is non-supporting then you can remove this fairly easily (however bear in mind there will be a lot of making good to do afterwards).

Stud walls or plasterboard walls are a simple timber stud frame construction covered with

An interior wall is often constructed of timber studs (above) with sheets of plasterboard nailed to it. Whether your wall is framed or solid will affect how you screw things to it.

plasterboard. The plasterboard is then skimmed with a layer of finishing plaster and then painted according to your decorative tastes.

Solid walls can be made of brickwork and may be screed in concrete. This type of construction can make it very difficult to screw into the wall. The load-bearing weight of a solid wall is more than that of a stud wall, so if you have something very heavy to hang then it's worth thinking about putting it on a solid wall.

Also note that above your windows there will be a **'lintel'** (see Glossary page 132) that supports the weight of the wall above the window. These are usually steel or brick and can be very difficult to drill in to. To combat this, it is common practice to hang a batten to the wall above the window and fix blinds or curtains to this batten (see 'Fitting a batten', page 48).

Windows have concrete or metal lintels.

FLOOR COVERINGS

The construction of your floors will depend on the age and style of your property. If you are in an older property, your floors are likely to be wood floorboards on top of a timber frame structure. In newer properties, however, the floors may well be concrete. Whatever your sub-layer, you have many floor covering options available to you. When making a choice about flooring, budget is probably one of the largest considerations; any of these flooring options can range from cheap to very, very expensive.

✔ Carpet is nice and warm under foot, keeps the heat in, but can look tired and jaded if not maintained properly. As well as wool and synthetic carpets, there are lovely designs made from grass. Grass grows fast and is happy being harvested.

✔ Sea grass grows in tropical climates on the banks of rivers. The natural fibre is harvested by hand, dried and hand-spun into cords before being woven into flooring.

✔ Traditional floorboards look beautiful and are nice to restore as an original feature; however they can be drafty in an old house.

✔ Amtico® is the king of plastic tiles. There is an excellent choice of styles and some are more expensive than wood. Hard-wearing and luxurious, Amtico tiles will last for many years.

✔ Marmoleum® is a revival of the old linoleum. Eco-friendly since it is made from resin and linseed oil with a jute backing, it is also good for allergy sufferers as it doesn't 'off-gas' (give off nasty toxic fumes). Available as tiles and rolls of solid flooring.

✔ Rubber can look a bit industrial but comes in some very funky colours and interesting textural designs; really suits a small bathroom or kitchen.

WATER, WATER EVERYWHERE

Mains water coming into a domestic property can be either direct or indirect. To tell which one you have, you will need to look at the type of hot water system you have. You are likely to have an **'indirect'** water system if you have a cold water storage tank (usually in your loft). The water comes into the property through a mains pipe and gets fed to the cold water tap in the kitchen and into a cold water storage tank, which in turn will feed all the other taps, showers and toilets.

If you have combination boiler (COMBI) or an unvented 'Megaflow' system, then the mains water entry is considered to be 'direct'. You are able to have hot water instantly and don't need to wait for a tank to fill. This means all the cold taps, showers, kitchen/laundry appliances, toilets etc. are fed water directly from the mains, at mains water pressures.

Many modern properties utilize a **'direct'** system, which has the advantage of minimizing the amount of plumbing required in the loft space and also means that showers and taps operate at a greater pressure – ideal if you prefer a really powerful shower. The main advantage to an 'indirect' system is that you are not without some water supply if there is a temporary mains failure and the water is shut off for a time.

✔ Solid wood floors can be laid over any levelled floor and can really change the look of the room. There is lots of choice and price range too.

✔ Engineered floors involve a surface of real wood veneer being applied to an interior of softwood ply. Bamboo is also available as a composite flooring alternative, a fast-growing resource with a variety of finishes.

✔ Laminate floors have a surface that is a photograph of wood printed on to a thin MDF board. It is easy to damage and impossible to repair. This option is quite cheap but the style is rather dated now.

✔ Bamboo flooring is one of the hardest natural materials available. Because bamboo is a rapid-growing grass and not a wood, it can be harvested every 3–5 years, unlike 15-25 years for most wood. This makes bamboo a very environmentally friendly product for flooring.

✔ Ceramic tiles are easy to clean but can be cold unless you install underfloor heating; these are best used in wet areas (kitchens, bathrooms and conservatories) but can be used anywhere.

✔ Vinyl floors are not as cheap and nasty as you might think; some really funky colours and options are available these days. Get a good-quality type – it will last a long time and won't look cheap.

Plumbing systems

If you have a plumbing disaster in your home the worst thing you can do is panic and the best thing you can do is be prepared. First of all you need to know what sort of system you have – indirect or direct. In an indirect cold water system (right) the cold water is stored in a tank normally kept in the roof and feeds nearly all the water outlets in the house, whereas in a direct cold water system (below), all cold water outlets are fed directly from the mains water suppply and so have mains pressure.

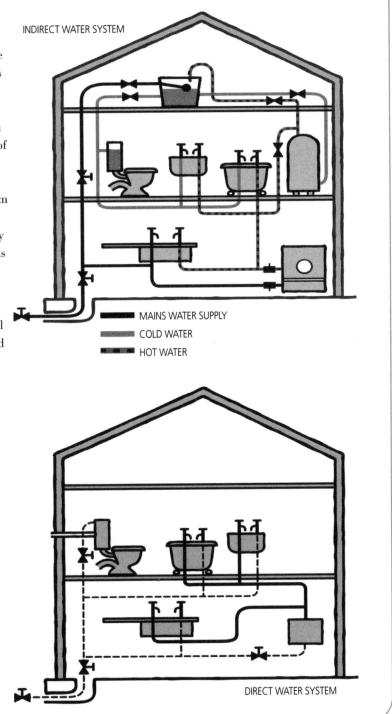

INDIRECT WATER SYSTEM

MAINS WATER SUPPLY
COLD WATER
HOT WATER

DIRECT WATER SYSTEM

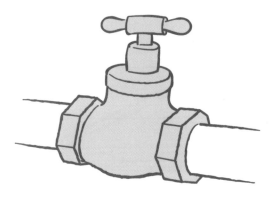

YOUR STOP COCK WILL LOOK SOMETHING LIKE THIS.

Stop cocks

Before disaster strikes, find out where your **stop cock** is and if it works. Make sure you know where all your important stop cocks are, because in a plumbing crisis, you will need to stop water coming into your property immediately. The best way to do this is to turn off your stop cock.

The stop cock isolates (shuts off) the mains water supply from the water that runs through your home. If you are in a flat this may be in a communal area such as the hallway, but in most properties it is located near the first source of mains water (usually the kitchen sink taps). It's important to locate and test your stop cock, because if you have a leak you will want to isolate the source of water coming into the property. By turning off the stopcock you will stop any further water from coming in to the property, thereby limiting any further damage from a leak.

As stop cocks are often left unused for years, they can frequently seize up and are unable to turn, so it's a good idea to find this out before an emergency strikes. This is a life saver – and can save you an awful lot of money on an emergency plumber. SO put down this book now, yes now, and find your stop cock. Turn it clockwise to turn it off, anti-clockwise for on.

If a stop cock hasn't been used in a while it can be really stiff, so spray a bit of lubricating oil in the joints, leave for 10 minutes to let it work its magic and you should be able to turn the valve. If you can't, then you'll need to get the valve replaced. It's best to find out now and get it replaced before you actually need it in an emergency.

Replacing a stop cock is a specialist job for an experienced plumber. It will involve freezing pipework or turning the water off in the street. Outside any property is a mains water stop cock that can be accessed through small panels in the street – you would need a special key to turn this; it's probably something you won't want to tackle yourself, especially if you are in a flat as you will be turning off the water to the whole building.

Pipework

Inside your property is a series of copper pipes that carries the water around and feeds it to different appliances, such as your shower or toilet. It might be sensible to make sure that each appliance has its own 'isolation valve' or mini stop cock (it's also known as a service valve).

This will allow the water to any appliance to be isolated and work can take place without having to shut off the mains water. This is very handy if you find you have a leaky toilet or shower as you can turn this valve on and off to limit damage and wasted water until the leak is fixed.

The copper pipes running through the house will carry cold water in one set and hot water in another. Cold water will be directed to your hot water system (boiler or tank) and then it will come out into a separate set of pipes that carries hot water around the property.

Waste pipes

Waste water is carried away from plumbing fixtures through large plastic pipes to the mains drainage system...and from there no one needs to know!

ELECTRICAL SYSTEM

Although we take it for granted, electricity is a complex system that needs a level of understanding before we can safely make any electrical changes to our homes. So how does it work?

Electricity is made in an power plant where fossil fuels (such as coal) are used to turn water into steam. This steam powers a turbine that spins a big magnet inside a copper wire. This heat energy is converted to mechanical energy that is then converted to electrical energy – SIMPLE!

From the power plant, the electric current runs through the power lines to a substation, then to an underground transformer or pylon. From here electricity comes into your home through a service box, where your meter is located to measure how much you use. Wires take electricity around your home powering your lights and all your other electrical appliances. There are multiple power circuits in your home, usually separated into lighting and power. There may also be separate supplies to appliances that require a lot of current.

 ## *Electrical safety issues*

Because of the obvious safety issues, there are many electrical tasks you should not do yourself. Remember tampering with electrics can be very dangerous if you don't know what you are doing. The section on projects outlines some safe things you can take on.

There are many restrictions on what electrical work you can do yourself and there's a good reason for this – poor electrics can and have caused serious fires. This is one area of health and safety that should be taken extremely seriously.

If you are not sure what work you can do yourself, then check with your local building regulations office. When getting someone in to complete certain electrical work for you, that person should provide you with a certificate at the end of the work detailing what has been completed. This certificate will also be stored with thier professional

registration body. If you don't have this certificate then the work is invalid and may even be fitted to illegal standards. This in turn could affect your insurance coverage, so ensure that your contractor provides you with this certificate at the end of the job where appropriate. Don't pay the bill until you've got it. You will especially need this certificate if you decide to rent out your property and also when you are selling your house.

Trade secret

Universal method for tightening and loosening: clockwise to tighten and anti-clockwise to loosen. Or remember: 'Righty Tighty-Lefty Loosey'.

Fuse box

Your fuse box no longer has fuses in it; instead it holds MCBs (Miniature Circuit Breakers) and an RCD (Residual Circuit Breaker) which isolate the source of electricity much like the stop cock and service valves in the plumbing system. From here, the wiring is taken to each room of the house and isolated by switches in the walls or on each appliance.

Fuses

Fuses come in a number of varieties but the ones you will be familiar with are the little glass vials that sit within a plug. A fuse is a metal wire that melts when too much current flows through a circuit – interrupting the circuit to which the item is connected. When a fuse blows, an interruption to the circuit occurs that prevents overheating and fire.

If an appliance doesn't work, it's worth changing the fuse to see if this is the problem. Use a screwdriver to unscrew the two sections of a plug and you will see the fuse sitting neatly in between two clips. Replace this with a new fuse of the same amp (the amp is written on the fuse) and screw the plug back together. Often that will solve the problem.

It's also worth checking what the fuse rating for the appliance is, as the item may be blowing due to having the wrong fuse.

ALL TOOLED UP

Before you can launch yourself into your DIY projects, you will need to acquire a basic tool kit and also learn a little about the materials you can expect to have to buy and use in the course of doing the projects.

Think of these items as 'empower' tools. Dodgy old blunt tools, discarded by others will not instill confidence so take yourself seriously and gather a basic box of tools to which you can add later. Most tools cost less than a bit of make-up kit and some cost as much as a pair of shoes but could last a lifetime and save a fortune.

Without tools, you will find it difficult to carry out the simplest tasks. If you are camping you can cook food with a stick and an open fire, but we all know how much easier it is to cook with a range of utensils and it's the same with DIY. If you know what tools you have AND WHERE THEY ARE, you can plan the job and do it whenever you find the time.

When setting up a basic tool kit, buy the best you can afford, but also acquire the ones

Containers for everything

Boxes, old tins with lids, plastic containers with lids and jam jars are just some of the possibilities for storage. You will need containers for:

✔ Screws, nails and drill bits. A plastic box with separate compartments works well for these but SORT THEM OUT. Keep the different sizes apart so you don't have to sort through every screw to find the size you want.

✔ Wall plugs. Depending on how many you gather, you can use a box or a bag for these.

✔ Keep old jam jars and jewellery boxes for screws and nails, stick a nail through the top so you know what size is in each jar or box before you open it.

you like. More expensive tools tend to give better performance than cheaper tools and may last longer, but if you only need a tool for one job and you know you won't use it again then it can't hurt to buy a cheaper version. Learn what each one does by practising with it before a big project if possible, and read its instructions.

Trying each one out and really getting familiar with them will give you more confidence when you use them for real. Every tool is designed to do a specific job, so use a tool in the way it was designed and it will make the job run more smoothly. A sure way to damage a tool is to use it for a job it's not designed to do.

A basic tool kit

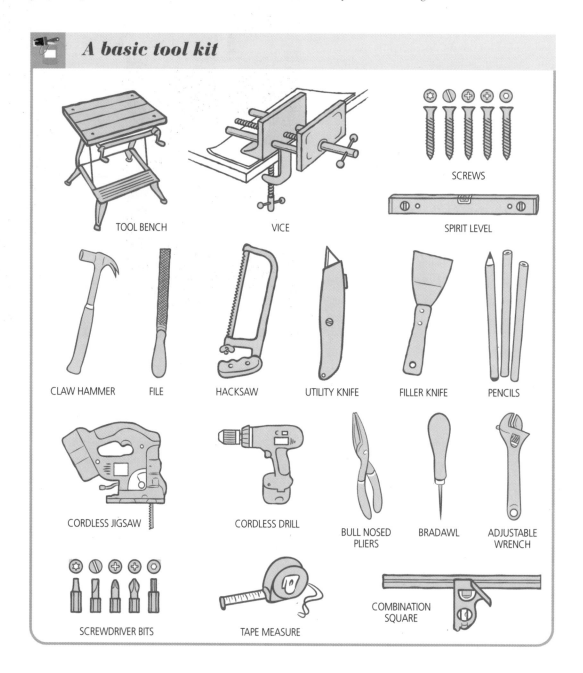

TOOL BENCH

VICE

SCREWS

SPIRIT LEVEL

CLAW HAMMER

FILE

HACKSAW

UTILITY KNIFE

FILLER KNIFE

PENCILS

CORDLESS JIGSAW

CORDLESS DRILL

BULL NOSED PLIERS

BRADAWL

ADJUSTABLE WRENCH

SCREWDRIVER BITS

TAPE MEASURE

COMBINATION SQUARE

✔ Use cut-down plastic milk containers or old jam jars for cleaning brushes.

✔ Old toothbrushes make great cleaners to boldly go where you don't want to...

✔ Old, chipped mugs are great to use as small paint kettles when doing small touch-ups.

✔ Artists' paint brushes are great for delicate paint areas or getting dust out of tight spaces.

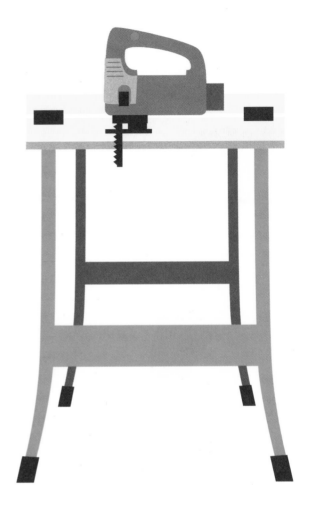

Where to buy

Think of choosing tools as you would choose a kettle – there's a lot of choice with regard to colour, material and design but ultimately it just boils water! Good places to browse are catalogues from online tool supply companies or your local mid-sized hardware store.

The advantage of buying from a hardware shop or DIY outlet is that you can ask a lot of questions. Ask the assistant to show you how to change a blade on a hacksaw, for instance. Watching someone do it is the best way to learn. Once you know what to look for, you can also pick up tools from market stalls and car boot sales.

Where to put your tools

A place for everything and everything in its place. You're all set to go, but where is that screwdriver and hammer? Start keeping everything together. Shoe boxes can hold your tools until you expand your collection and then the shoe box can hold all the clips, staples, spare blades etc.

Good tool storage places include under the stairs, in the bottom of a cupboard in a special box or in a trunk doubling as a coffee table. I'm sure that there are any number of places in your home where tools can be stored out of sight.

If you invest in a tool box make sure it's big and sturdy enough for you. A tool box isn't just great

storage but in a pinch you can also use it as a mini workbench, and you can stand and sit on it if you don't have a stepladder around.

The work place

A **foldable work bench** is the right height for working at, will hold your wood tightly while you work and is a fabulous friend that will keep your furniture from being ruined. There are several lightweight adjustable, foldable workbenches on the market that fit into the back of a cupboard. If you can't find room for a bench then don't despair; buy a removable table vice and attach it to a worktop or a table when needed. Use a section of cardboard to protect the surface of the table and make it secure with masking tape.

MEASURING AND MARKING TOOLS

'Measure twice, cut once' so the saying goes. I'll add my own tip – measure it again if you have taken a tea break before cutting it. Also mark the section to be kept and the section to be discarded so that you will know which is which. But in order to measure you need the right tools:

✔ Five-metre (16 ft) retractable tape. Try some out in the shop – unroll it and see how long you can unreel it till it 'breaks' (bends). The longer the tape the better and very handy if you are measuring things by yourself. It should have clear readable numbers that you can understand.

✔ Combination square. This is used for marking right angles, perpendicular marks and 45° angles. Look for clear measurements on the straight part. Most have a small pin that unscrews and can be used for scribing (scratching the line to be marked).

✔ Spirit level. Used for checking and marking horizontal and vertical lines. Look for easy-to-read 'bubbles', both horizontal and vertical. Long versions can also be used as a straight edge to cut against. Smaller ones can be used as a plumb line too.

✔ Pencil. SHARPNESS is the key to accuracy. Ask yourself 'What side of the pencil line am I cutting against?' Buy two wide, flat 'carpenter's pencils. They are oval in shape so that when you put them down they don't roll way. Buy two because a pencil's main aim in life is to hide from you during a project.

✔ Bradawl. Like a very small screwdriver, but used for making a very small hole in wood. This is called a 'pilot' hole before drilling a bigger hole. It makes the hole more accurate and well worth the extra step. Look for a comfortable handle – some have a flat head, some have a square rod.

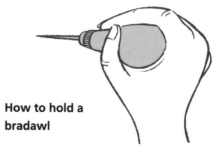

How to hold a bradawl

✔ Mitre box. This useful device will help guide you to cut small lengths of wood at angles when finishing a wooden floor.

CUTTING TOOLS

There are an assortment of tools for cutting various materials, so you will need several tools to accomplish the cutting you will do.

✔ Utility knife/all-purpose cutting knife and a set of spare blades. This is an invaluable tool for cutting vinyl tiles and carpet and for scoring lines. It is also brilliant for sharpening pencils. Look for a sturdy well-fitting handle; the blade should not rattle when the screw is tightened. Learn how to replace the blade.

✔ Junior hacksaw with a set of replaceable blades. A non-powered option for cutting small pieces of wood, especially if you have to hold it near the edge. Also brilliant for cutting curtain track, plastic pipe, dowel and carpet strip. It won't cut anything larger than the distance between the blade and the back. Look for a fairly comfortable handle. Learn how to change the blade since it becomes blunt eventually, and too much exertion may make the blade snap. It's OK – this is normal. Practise changing the blade when you aren't in a hurry – it's a technique that requires pressure against the saw handle.

✔ Hacksaw and set of replaceable blades. Look for a fairly comfortable handle.

Hold the saw firmly and level and stand square on to the work you are cutting. It helps to keep the cut vertical. Holding your first finger straight against the saw will help to keep it steady (see below).

✔ Electric powered jigsaw. Look for a bigger motor (18v) since the more it will cut through like butter, the less sweat you will produce. Cordless tools make working up a ladder and in the garden more convenient but are heavier. However, working with these will have a beneficial effect on any bingo wings. The speed needs to be variable so you can cut fast for wood and very slow for metal (it gets hot). The base plate can be adjusted to cut at 45° angles so it can cut moulding and frames. If it can collect the sawdust then less mess for you to clear up and if it has a laser guide for cutting it's about perfect. Get an assortment of blades – a pack of 'rough cut', a pack of 'fine cut' and a pack for metal cutting.

✔ A set of pliers. Flat nose, round nose, saw nose will be plenty to start. These are extra hands to help hold and cut wire and cable.

NAILING AND SCREWING IMPLEMENTS

✔ Claw hammer. For nailing and removing nails. Look for a firm head and a very fine V in the claw for removing nails. The flat face should be gently rounded to not dent the surface of the wood when driving nails home. Heavy is good. Remember that the weight of a tool can make up for the lack of muscle strength.

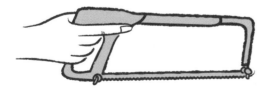

How to hold a hacksaw

How to hold a hammer

pincers in one hand and pliers in the other for an effective method of undoing or unscrewing objects – very Edward Scissorhands.

✔ Ratchet screwdriver. Helps keep the screwdriver in the head of the screw, helps to make the turn and doesn't waste muscle power when turning the screwdriver the other way. The ratchet device operates to both screw and unscrew and can be 'locked' to operate as an ordinary screwdriver.

✔ Cordless electric screwdriver. It's a fab toy. Buy a good one with a long battery life – it will save time and muscle and are vital for Flat-pack Queens.

✔ Set of assorted screwdriver bits. A set will have slot heads, cross heads as well as a hex head to assemble flat-pack furniture fast.

DRILLING TOOLS

✔ Cordless drill with a 'keyless' chuck. The BEST thing in a girl's tool kit. It is heavier than a drill with a cord, but fabulously freeing when up a ladder or walking across a room – you won't need to use an extension lead. Not only will it drill all the holes you will ever need, you can also use it as a really powerful screwdriver, though I recommend that you have an additional cordless screwdriver (see above) if you are planning a big project so you won't have to change bits from drills to screwdriver heads

✔ Smaller ball/pein hammer. (pein or peen – it's a metal worker thing...). It's used for starting nails and pins on intricate jobs. Look for lighter but still firmly fixed head.

✔ Nail sets. Steel instrument used for hammering in nails below the surface.

✔ Pincers. Used for removing nails. You can use

Terrified of using a drill?

Are you terrified of hairdryers? Unlikely. Terrified of a food mixer? Even less likely. A drill uses a rotary motor (it makes things go round) and you hold it like a hairdryer. Go to a big hardware store that has plenty on display and pick some up and point them away from you. Go on – it won't hurt anything (they are not charged).

How to choose a drill? The same sort of choices as a hairdryer or a sewing machine – how much power you need, how many options do you want. Pick an amount you want to spend and buy one you can move all the switches on – remember some will feel stiff because they are designed to avoid getting knocked on or off accidentally. They do tend to be designed for bigger hands so you may have to reach a bit further but even very dainty paws manage to use drills.

The drill bits fit into the drill by gripping into the three jaws that open when the chuck tightens. Learn how to use it. Get it home and charge the battery like a mobile phone. You can play with it to learn what it does. Variable speeds mean you can cut metal slowly and ease your way through thick wood.

Buy an 18v drill if possible (use the power of the tool to compensate for lack of muscle strength). Buy a 'combi' drill. This will have a 'hammer action' option and is brilliant for drilling into wall. Get one with two batteries. A battery may run down before a job is finished so it's handy to have a spare on charge.

✔ Set of drill bits. The spiral-bladed things that drill the holes are called bits. You need three set of bits: one for wood, one for metal and one for concrete/brick. Buying a complete set of drill bits means you know you have all the sizes you will ever need. The bits will blunt eventually, like pencils, and you can buy replacements individually as you go along. Expensive bits will be worth the money – they are sharper and will last longer. If you don't want screw heads to rest above the surface, then buy a countersink bit to use after drilling the hole.

SMOOTHING AND SHAPING TOOLS

✔ Sanding block.
Look for ones made from a wood block with felt on one side and a slit for securing the sandpaper. Others are made of hard rubber or cork. A block will ensure that the surface being sanded has constant pressure and is flat.

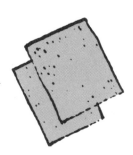

✔ Sandpaper. The grittiness is measured by number so 40 is very coarse and 240 is very fine. Buy an assorted pack and keep all the sheets together with the sanding block in a supermarket bag, then you aren't hunting for the block when you need it. If you are doing a lot of decorating, it's cheaper to buy sandpaper by the metre/yard from a trade store.

✔ Electric sander. Sheet sanders are easy to use – like using an iron from Mad Max. On some machines the sandpaper even attaches by VELCRO! Beware the orbital sander, as they are more likely to gouge into the wood and leave bad semi-circle memories. Small mouse sanders are great for getting into small places and look cute too.

✔ Files. Three assorted hand files with handles to smooth wood and metal. Round, triangular and flat in shape from rough to fine. The middle-size crosscut file is called a bastard. Keep a straight face when asking for one in a hardware shop.

To keep a straight edge when filing, stand behind the work and use long, smooth, even strokes. Files can be used to make fine adjustments to wood, great when you need to shave a thin area off a shelf or can be used to create channels for cables.

✔ Cold chisel. Not expensive but very empowering. You can remove tiles, flooring, skirting boards, stuff that's stuck with a cold chisel and a hammer. Often, the first tool on a job.

This list isn't comprehensive, but will enable you to assemble a set of tools to embark on many projects in this book. Beside the tools, there are various 'must have' items that can be used on almost any project.

How to hold a cold chisel

✔ Screws and nails. Buy assorted packs of screws and nails. These contain a selection of the most popular sizes. Until you begin a job, it's impossible to know what you will need. Cross-head screws are easier to use and require less muscle than traditional slotted head screws. There are lots of brands with 'Turbo' and 'Max' in the names. These are even easier to drive home (screw into material).

✔ Masking tape. Marvellous for holding down, light clamping, marking out on shiny objects, picking up annoying bits of sawdust off the floor and you. Remember to remove it or it will becme stickier and turn into MARKING tape.

GLUES AND SOLVENTS

✔ Cartridge gun. Cheaper and much easier to use than little tubes, the cartridge gun will apply sealant, glue and caulk quickly and with style, making you look and feel like a pro.

✔ Woodwork glue. Also called PVA glue (poly vinyl acetate). Wipe off excess quickly as it's harder to remove once it dries. Water solvent, PVA is like school glue so if you get any on your hands you may delight in peeling it away and revelling in school-day memories.

✔ Other glues. Invest in a pack of two-part epoxy glue, a tube of superglue and some impact adhesive. As you get in the DIY groove you can decide which is the best glue for a job.

✔ Grab adhesive. When you discover GRAB ADHESIVE, your confidence level will soar. This brilliant stuff is very viscous and very strong. It sticks everything to everything as well, so be careful when using it as you don't want to stick your clothes to your new shelves.

✔ Can of WD-40. (Water Displacement – 40th attempt). The inventor was a persistent guy. This versatile spray repels moisture and loosens things like squeaky doors and helps unstick overtightened joints.

✔ Can of orange-scented goo remover. Great for removing sticky labels and old stickers.

✔ White spirit. For cleaning oil-based paints from brushes and rollers.

✔ Washing-up liquid. An underrated DIY helper. It acts as a surfactant as it dissolves grease on contact. Add a teensy drop to paint where the area is too smooth (glass or shiny metal) to hold.

✔ Baby oil. Great for removing stubborn stains on skin and hard surfaces.

Special tools for specific uses

ELECTRICAL PROJECTS

✔ Insulated screwdrivers and pliers with a thick rubber handle to limit shocks.

✔ Stud/wire detector to check you aren't going to drill into cables.

✔ Small screwdrivers for connection boxes.

✔ Wire cutters.

✔ Rubber-soled shoes. You may thank the Earth one day...

PLUMBING PROJECTS

✔ WC Auger. No, not a romantic poet but a metal rod with a curly end for unblocking a toilet. It costs a fraction of what an emergency plumber will charge and may save friendships if you share a flat with someone who uses a roll of loo paper every day.

✔ PTFE tape. A special tape that works like a washer when fitting plastic pipes. It's special because it is both slippery and can grip. (Polytetrafluoroethylene, if you are scientifically minded...)

✔ Adjustable spanners. Preferably two so you can use them both for grip.

✔ A bucket and old rags. No matter how hard you try there will always be a spillage.

✔ Pipe cutter. A whizzy little tool that easily cuts closet rails and metal curtain rods when not being a plumber's mate.

✔ Hole saws for cutting holes for pipework.

TILING PROJECTS

✔ Tile spacers.

✔ Trowel or spatula to spread adhesive.

✔ Groat float or spatula.

✔ Tile cutters. Either hand-held like big scissors or bigger like a paper cutter.

✔ Nibbler. A type of pincers that will nibble away at a small amount of a tile.

MATERIAL GIRL

Since DIY projects use a variety of materials, you will need to get to know your way around a builder's merchant or your local DIY store. And while you are there you will want to look like you know what you are doing. Wood in all its many forms has different properties and you will need to pick the types to suit your needs. Read on...

Solid wood

Solid wood can be bought in various shapes, sizes and permutations. The upside of using wood is that it looks natural and is easy to join together; screws do not need wall fixings; and DIY shops sell lengths of soft woods in long lengths. The downsides are that wood has knots that are hard to drill and cut and it can continue to move or warp for years; natural soft wood will need sanding and finishing with stain or paint to make it moisture-proof.

MDF

Medium density fibreboard (MDF) has been around since the 1980s and quite simply, is mashed-up wood fibre held together with resin. Many online companies will cut and deliver shapes for you. The upside of using MDF is that it has no grain, it allows for a smooth finish to surfaces, is great for shelves and simple forms that do not have to be attached to each other, special screws will help hold pieces together; and it is less expensive than solid wood. The downside,

however, is that the resins contain urea formaldehyde which can cause irritation (wear goggles and respiratory mask when cutting and sanding); unless it is a special waterproof variety MDF will absorb moisture so takes longer to paint; it's harder to joint well as fibres are soft and will pull apart; it is heavier than decorative-faced particle board (see below) as the resin is heavy. Consider this when judging the span of a shelf.

Chipboard

Chipboard has a fairly smooth surface and is made from chips of wood held together with resin. The upside of chipboard is that it is less dense and less expensive than MDF. The downside, however, is that it requires a lot of finishing for a good effect; and it needs knock-down joints to hold it together.

Decorative-faced particle board™

A chipboard with a thin melamine surface, its cut edges can be finished by applying an iron-on edging, purchased separately. The upside of this board is that it is available in several different wood-effect finishes and white; the surfaces are water-resistant and wipeable. The downside of decorative-faced particle board, like with MDF, is its weakness if screwed into directly. Use special knock-down fittings to join surfaces or dowel joint it together.

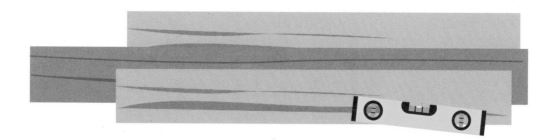

Buying wood or how to swagger in a timber yard

Some small local hardware shops carry a stock of pre-cut soft wood, mostly pine. It comes in a large variety of sizes. Browse the selection and make a note of the sizes available. These shops will often have a variety of cornicing or quarter-round beading used for finishing the edges of a floor when laying new flooring if you haven't removed the skirting boards. There is often a range of sizes that can be used as battens. These can also be used for slats for easy-to-make shelves inside cupboards. Round dowels can be used for small rails.

To make sure that the wood you are buying is straight and 'true', hold one end of the length and sight your eye down to the other end (see photograph above). Check both width and depth. If it has a bend or curve in it, put it back.

BASIC SKILLS

Mastering a few basic skills – measuring and cutting wood, joining two bits of wood together and drilling holes in walls – will mean that you can tackle a whole range of projects. But first things first.

JOINING PIECES OF WOOD TOGETHER

Once you have mastered the art of joining two pieces of wood/MDF/chipboard together, you can give free rein to your imagination and begin to create your own wonderful item. Use a square to make sure the boards are at right angles to each other. Opposite are three methods of joining two pieces of material together, ranging from the very easy to quite demanding.

Cutting wood down to size

First measure the board with a tape measure and mark a short line with a sharp pencil. Then measure it again, just to make sure. Remember to measure twice, cut once. If the board is wider than the combi square, measure in two places and use a long straight edge to mark the cutting line.

If you are using decorative-faced particle board, use masking tape to cover the area to be cut as this helps keep the melamine surface from chipping. **Cut the correct side of the pencil line.** The blade of the saw will remove some wood and that needs to be taken into account. Don't be tempted to measure lots of lengths from the

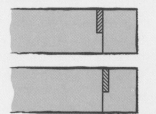

same board before cutting. Cut one piece then measure the next one. Avoid using one piece as a template as a form of Chinese whispers can ensure that the whole job becomes inaccurate. Use a **jigsaw and a straight edge** to cut the boards to size. Wait until you have assembled the piece before applying the decorative edges to decorative particle board in case the length needs adjusting.

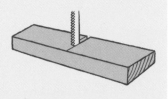

Point the saw in the direction you want the sawdust to end up. The vent in the saw blows a cascade in front of your work. Wear goggles so you don't waste time getting the flying sawdust out of your eye.

All joined up – putting it together

Using rigid joint blocks

You can use **rigid joint blocks** to join two pieces of material together – the easy option. These blocks are often made of plastic and have screw holes on both flat surfaces. Start by making sure that your boards are at right angles to each other. Place the rigid joint block at the inside joint and mark with a pencil where each screw hole needs to go. Start each screw hole with a bradawl and then using a cordless screwdriver, join the pieces together using the joint block and the screws. Use

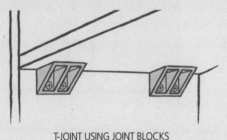

T-JOINT USING JOINT BLOCKS

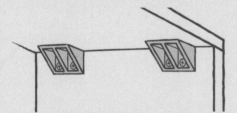

BUTT JOINT USING JOINT BLOCKS

screws with threads all the way up to the head and make sure the screws are shorter than the depth of the board. Note that the two illustrations above show a T-joint and a butt joint held together using rigid joint blocks.

Direct drilling joints

This method requires skill. If you don't mind seeing screw head marks on the surface of the board, mark the place where the joint is to be made and mark a centre line for the drill hole. Drill a hole through the side with a countersink bit, then hold the joint in place, and screw the two pieces of wood together. Finish the hole with filler or a purchased plastic cap. (The illustration below left is a butt joint using joint blocks; if you are using the direct drilling method, you would not use blocks, but would be making your drill mark on the top board and screwing from the top to join the top horizontal board to the vertical piece of wood.)

Dowel joints

Using **dowel rods** is an age-old and very skilled method for joining boards. If you are neat, patient and accurate, there is something very satisfying about the invisible way that dowels work. The skill is in the marking and drilling. Everything has to be aligned perfectly and at right angles. Use purchased dowels and the same size drill bit. Mark the ends of the board and transfer the marks to the corresponding surface using a combi square and pencil. The dowels are glued for extra security. You will need a sash clamp to hold the pieces together or wedge between furniture to dry. Make sure it is square before the glue dries.

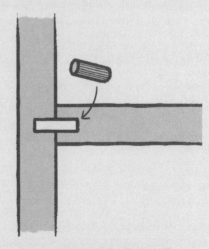

T-JOINT USING DOWEL JOINT

A TURNING POINT IN DIY SKILLS

This is it. Drilling! From this single skill mighty projects can grow. At first, a heavy picture can hang on a wall instead of lounging on the floor, and a shelf can hold books at last but after that? Fixing a batten and then a curtain? A closet? A stud wall? A house extension? OK, let's not run before we can walk.

A supported shelf uses several principles of physics. The shelf is on the outside of the wall while the screw acts as a cantilever inside. There are also forces pushing down on the shelf or bracket and back into the wall. All these factors dictate what will crash down in the middle of the night and what will hold the weight of of a ton of books. It is highly recommended that the largest and strongest fixing be used when possible.

Practise **playing with your drill** before starting a project if this is a new skill. Any new tool is like a new phone. Relax and get to know your drill until you can find your way around it with ease. You could even read the manual.

Fixing a screw into a wall

DIFFICULTY RATING

TIME FRAME
This will depend on what the screw is designed to hold, but roughly 30 minutes.

YOU WILL NEED
Pencil
Bradawl
Drill
Drill bits
Plastic wall fixings
Hammer
Screwdriver
Screws
Masking tape
Paper envelope
Spirit level

There are two basic kinds of wall: solid brickwork or concrete blocks with plaster on surface and hollow timber frame (stud walls) covered by plasterboard or plaster on laths. Knock on a wall with your knuckles. If it hurts, it's probably brick, if it makes a hollow sound, it's probably...hollow. Knock along a whole wall and listen carefully for changes in the sound. Studs will run from top to bottom of the wall about 40 cm (16 inches) or 60 cm (24 inches) apart.

Unless the wall is made of wood, a screw placed directly into the wall will have no strength. If the wall is brick, a screw will not secure in the dust and will be easy to pull out. If it is hollow, white plaster dust will give way to air, and anything directly screwed into the wall will loosen. To make a strong hold into the wall, the screw must be screwed into a plastic plug (fixing) that is fitted into a drilled hole.

Drilling the hole

When you have measured or decided where the hole is to be made, use a sharp pencil to mark the spot with an 'X'. It's easier to locate an X on a wall and is more accurate than a round blob of a spot. Yes, I have drilled a hole where a fly had marked the wall instead of my tiny pencil mark.

Use a bradawl to make a small hole in the exact centre of the X mark. This is a hugely beneficial piece of preparation as it will stop the drill skidding and will make the hole more accurate. If you are drilling into brickwork or concrete, place a length of masking tape over the approximate position and mark on top of that. If that won't stick to the surface, use a china marker/chalk in a contrasting colour. Use masking tape to tape an **open envelope** under where the hole will be. This will catch all the debris and dust as it falls out of the hole and make clearing up a breeze (see below).

When attaching shelves, blinds or rails to the wall, place the item on the wall where you want it to be fixed and mark the position of the screw holes with a sharp pencil or a bradawl. Make sure it is level by using a spirit level if necessary. Wonky won't do.

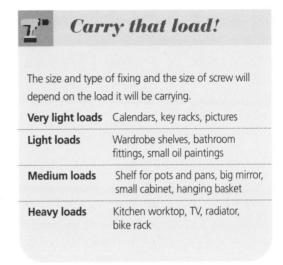

Carry that load!

The size and type of fixing and the size of screw will depend on the load it will be carrying.

Very light loads	Calendars, key racks, pictures
Light loads	Wardrobe shelves, bathroom fittings, small oil paintings
Medium loads	Shelf for pots and pans, big mirror, small cabinet, hanging basket
Heavy loads	Kitchen worktop, TV, radiator, bike rack

What size hole?

The choice of fixing will dictate the size and depth of the hole. The hole must be deep enough for the fixing to fit 'flush' to the surface. The bigger and heavier the thing to be attached, the bigger and deeper the hole. Not sure what you are drilling into? Then start small.

Drilling a pilot hole

Drilling a very small hole (known as a pilot hole) will help ensure accuracy and save time in the long run. Use a small masonry bit and drill a pilot hole. Take the drill and gently place it on the tiny hole made by the bradawl. Turn the drill on –- a variable speed drill will get up to speed slowly as you press harder on the trigger. Hold the drill firmly and make sure it is level. This is easier if you are drilling at about eye-level or shoulder height.

If the drill produces white dust then gives into free space, it's a hollow wall. If the wall resists the drill a little and brick or cement dust emerges, it's solid. By making the small hole first, the hole is drilled as a gradual process and will be a lot more accurate and easier to do. Remember, if you don't have muscles then rely on the tools. Choose a wall fixing suitable for the wall and load. Read the pack for guidance.

What fixing and how to choose

Some items such as blinds and curtain rails arrive with little packages containing screws and wall fixings. Inspect them closely and regard with great suspicion. Often they are of inferior quality. Hardware stores sell a variety of designs and manufacturers never stop competing for the Holy Grail of perfect wall fixing. Call me when you find it.

Buy a pack of assorted sizes of fixings for hollow and solid walls. When you drill into a wall you will find out more about the substrate and you will already have the answer in your tool box. READ THE PACK instructions. Packs of fixings clearly state what type of wall they are designed for and all have the correct drill size and range of screw sizes that can be used printed on the packaging. If you are a knitter you will be familiar with the wraps around the yarn that suggests the needle and tension size.

For heavier objects in hollow walls, use a toggle type of fixing with wings or collapsible anchor type. These have an expanding plug that remains in place if the screw is removed. They work by opening as the screw or bolt is tightened.

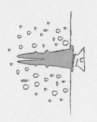

Solid wall fixing

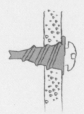

Hollow wall screw-in fixing

Hollow wall wings fixing

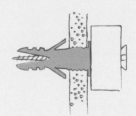

All-in-one fixing for solid or hollow wall

Drill as deep as the fixing. There is no point in drilling deeper than necessary so wrap a small piece of masking tape around the drill bit as a depth gauge. This is also a good idea if you are part-drilling into a piece of wood and don't want to drill right through. Place the fixing against the drill bit and mark the depth of hole required with a small piece of masking tape wrapped around the bit.

If you have a combi drill, use the 'hammer' action on the drill if drilling into cement or brick. The drill knocks forward and back while it is drilling and makes a satisfying growling noise. This is essential if you are hanging a bracket for a hanging basket or an extendable washing line on an outside wall. This setting isn't necessary if drilling into wood or plaster.

Keep the drill running while slowly removing occasionally while you are drilling. This will pull all the debris out and make sure the drill is clean. Try to keep your hand steady, since too much wobbling will make the hole too big. When the hole is drilled and clear, gently tap the fixing into the wall with a hammer. If the fixing is tight and flush with the wall, your work is done. Use the screw size recommended on the wall fixing pack. These usually supply a range of length and thicknesses that can be used. The screw should be as long as possible for greater strength.

Choosing the screw

The choices and properties extolled by screw companies are like the myriad options when choosing a toothbrush or razor. They are available in double thread, turbo max, gold plus tip cutting blah blah, but for the majority of simple tasks, a hardened metal countersunk wood screw will do the job. Some are self-tapping, which means they do not require a pilot hole to be drilled first. The advantage of using a designer screw is that they will often bite in easier and require less muscle.

Once you have mastered placing a screw

Screw sizes

Screws are measured by gauge (diameter of shank) and length. Popular gauge sizes are: 6 for hinges and catches; 8 for light doors and shelves; 10 for external doors and heavy work. Lengths are measured from end of thread to surface and are available from 6 mm to 150 mm (¼ inch to 6 inches). Use as large a screw as you can for extra strength. Remember that the length of screw will include the measurement of the batten or bracket as well as the depth of plastic fixing.

into a wall you have got to grips with a core skill for tackling many of the projects in this book. Finally, screw the hardware – toilet roll holder, key rack or batten into the wall. Pat yourself on the back.

GLUING STUFF TO THE WALL

There are some absolutely amazing bonding adhesives available and sometimes they can take the place of (or supplement) a nail or screw in a wall. The bond is only as good as the surface it is sticking to so if you glue something to a flaky wall, the flakes will stick to the glue and the flakes will fall off. Paint may separate from plaster, wallpaper may come loose from the wall, so don't expect to cheat the laws of nature. Make sure that the surfaces are dust-free and dry. Glue will not stick to a greasy surface.

 ## *Trade secret*

If the hole you have drilled is slightly too big and the fixing isn't tight, push a matchstick or three into the hole to make it slightly smaller and try the fixing again. This isn't a mad bodge solution, it's a trick that many builders use all the time. If you can't make the hole deep enough and you can't try in a different place on the wall, mix a little fast-setting two-part epoxy glue to fill the hole and pack with matchsticks. Then use a shorter, thicker screw. Remember though, that this will not be as strong as a well-fitting hole and wall fixing.

Hot glue

A hot glue gun is a great way to hold small lightweight items. It is not so good over a large area as the glue quickly cools and loses its stickiness. Work quickly and in small areas at a time. Hot glue will always remain somewhat flexible so it can't be used to fill holes where a screw is going to be inserted.

Nail-substitute glue

Often these glues come in handy tubes to use with a cartridge gun. Lock and load the tube and cut off the tip. These glues are great for gluing uneven surfaces and will fill fairly big gaps so can hold up skirting boards and cornices. Because they are so viscous and dry quite quickly, the work will not slide while it is wet. BUT tape it or hold it in place if you think it may move. Once it is dry it is very difficult to remove so take care. It can also be used for additional strength when attaching a batten.

Velcro™

Don't dismiss this haberdashery staple. Hook and loop tape is available with a sticky back and can hold items on a wall up to about the weight of an iron. Use larger thicker strips to maximize hold.

Sticky pads

If you use sticky-backed hooks to hold light items such as tea towels, taking a little bit of time will produce a neat result. Use a spirit level if you are aligning more than one hook and wash and dry the surface first to remove any grease. This is an optimum solution in a rented property as hooks can be removed by gently inserting 'goo remover' behind fixing and slowly wiggling it free. Wipe off excess with more goo remover.

PART II: Projects

Now we can begin to have fun! After an overview of basic tools and skills, we can embark on combining some of those skills to achieve an endless number of personalized DIY solutions. Be guided by our difficulty rating system, but jump in if you feel more confident. Gather your tools, materials and courage and launch forth.

GETTING IT UP

One of the most frustrating aspects of not being able to DO IT YOURSELF is revealed when you go shopping. There to tantalize you is a lovely toilet roll holder and matching towel rack but you don't know how to get those items on to your wall unless some handy person comes by. Instead you buy another free-standing item to add to already crowded shelves. Shelves? (We will go there later.)

It's all about loading. How heavy is the item you are trying to hang? Let's start with a toilet roll holder. As long as you aren't trying to lift yourself up by it, it doesn't need to be hung on the wall by anything more than the wall fixings mentioned in 'What fixing and how to choose' (see page 40). The same goes for a coat or towel hook – with two fixings and screws the right length, the weight of what is normally hung there will not pull the hook off the wall.

However, a roller blind or curtains will need some more thought. Not only does the fixing need to support the weight of the blind or curtain and poles, it will need to bear the extra stress when the curtains are opened and closed, or when the cat climbs up them. Read on and all will be revealed!

Hanging a blind or curtain

YOU WILL NEED

Step ladder
Drill and drill bits
Spirit level
Pencil
Screws
Wall fixings
Mastic gun
Nail substitute glue
Batten
Sandpaper
Bradawl
Masking tape

BATTEN ATTACHED ABOVE A WINDOW

Depending on where the blind is to be hung, several screws holding the bracket in place might suffice. If the blind is being secured onto a wooden window frame then it need not be held by wall fixings, but secured directly into the wood. If the blind is to be recessed into a window alcove, the brackets will be fixed directly into the plaster wall above or either side of the window.

If the blind or pole is to be fixed directly above the window, there may be a metal or cement lintel or beam that provides support across the window. This can be very difficult to drill into and often a wooden batten fixed onto the wall using screws and nail substitute glue will provide a much stronger solution (see illustration).

Drilling above a window is fraught with surprises, besides the above mentioned lintel. In older houses there is a complete void! The drill finds a cavity inside the plaster when trying to make a pilot hole. All these reasons point toward the fitting of a batten (see page 35 about buying wooden battens).

FITTING A BATTEN

Decide where the top of the curtains will be. Measure the length of the blind or pole and add

10 cm (4 inches) so that the brackets won't be attached right at the end of the wood where it may split. Mark the required length on the batten with a square and after measuring TWICE, cut it using a jigsaw or small hacksaw. Finish the wood with fine sandpaper to remove splinted wood at the end.

Use a spirit level to make a fine pencil line along the bottom of where the batten will be fixed. As it is up high, it's easier to mark the underside rather than the top line. Consider how many screws to fit – as few as possible since we are busy people, but enough to hold the weight.

Drill three or more holes (5mm /¼ inch bit) evenly spaced along the batten. These holes will take the screws and are used to mark the position of any drilling into the wall. If you don't drill a

hole through the wood, the screw will split it.

Position the batten against the pencil line and mark the centre hole through the batten holes. If you have an accomplice they can hold the wood length while you mark all the holes, but as the wood can slip when you are working alone, drill and fix the middle screw first and then mark and drill the rest of the holes once you have one in place to hold itself level.

When the wood has been marked with the centre hole, fit an appropriate wall fixing (see 'What fixing' page 40). Then place a screw into the batten and tighten into the wall. Now mark the wall through the rest of the holes using the bradawl with the batten level against the pencil line. Loosen the holding screw so that the batten rotates slightly and reveals the marks. Drill into the marks and fit wall fixings. Rotate the batten back to level and tighten onto wall with the remaining screws.

If there isn't any chance of being able to screw into a wall or even a part of the depth because there is a restriction and a drill won't fit, a combination of glue and screws can be used.

If using ONLY nail substitute glue, bear in mind that it will need to be held in place until the glue sets. If so, pre-drill small pilot holes in batten and tap a nail through. The batten can be held temporarily by the nails that can just grip the wall surface, even if it's concrete. Use long nails and leave the heads above the wood so that they can be removed easily once the glue has set.

The batten can now be painted the same colour as the wall and once the curtain pole or blind has been fitted, will hardly be visible.

Some blinds and poles are quite heavy, particularly wooden or metal ones, so use the longest screws possible to hold the pole in place. The length will be decided by the maximum depth you can screw into. Decide the size of the wall fixing first.

GETTING A HANDLE ON HOME SECURITY

There is something thrilling about closing the door of your own place, whether it's the door to a flat, a house or just a room of your own. But once you're in, how do you make sure that the only people who come in are people you invite? There are several easy ways to beef up your security without resorting to bars on the windows. If the place isn't your own and you would still like more security, ask your landlord for permission to add some safety features. They may even pay for the hardware as it will remain with the property. If they won't, then consider adding a keyless door lock – the sort used on hostels and hotel rooms; it's removable and does not require elaborate fitting.

Locks, bolts and spyholes

TIME FRAME

Allow 1 hour for each small project

YOU WILL NEED

Measuring tape
Pencil
Screwdriver sets
Variable-speed drill
Drill bits
Additional locks and security devices

DOORS

The front door into your property will probably be the strongest and the one that needs to be the most secure. If you have a garden or balcony door make sure these have excellent security as well. Check the existing lock on the door and if possible get another set of keys cut to leave with a family member or reliable neighbour. Check that it has all the screws fitted and that these are fully tightened. Make sure that the latch fits into the door frame and can't be forced from the outside.

Deadbolt lock A simple deadbolt can be fitted as an extra safety feature. It will also help to stop the door rattling and scaring the bejesus out of you at night. Make sure it is fitted as far away from the door glass, if there is any, so that prying hands can't undo it.

Spy hole A spy hole or door viewer offers a wide field of vision to ensure that you have the best opportunity to identify your visitor before deciding whether to open the door or not. Most spy holes are designed for use in doors up to 50 mm (2 inches) thick and only require drilling a 12 mm (½ inch) hole to install. Centre the spy hole by measuring the width of the door and halving it.

Door guard Bogus callers who use distraction

burglary techniques don't like door chains or door guards since these offer an opportunity to observe a visitor face-to-face without giving them access to your property. This is a vital deterrent to an intruder. Door guards are a better alternative than a door chain as the solid construction has more strength than a chain and offers less chance of being opened by a smaller hand. Use long steel screws and follow the directions on the fitting.

Safety chain and mirror Safety chains can be fitted to the inside of the door and do not require

specialist equipment. Remember to use the longest screws possible and make sure that the distance between the lock and the fitting place for the chain is as far apart as possible. Door chain mirrors are a really simple addition to your door if visibility is restricted when you use a door chain. A small mirror can be stuck onto the door frame, making it possible to see the visitor without removing the chain.

WINDOWS

Locks can also be fitted to every type of window for added security.

Sash windows

Locks can be fitted onto the wooden part of sash windows. They work by immobilizing the window into which the lock has been installed – a bolt is screwed to the outer sash that passes over the top of the inner sash so both windows are secure.

To let some fresh air in but nothing else, place the bolt about 10 cm (4 inches) lower than the closed level of the window. This way, the window can be opened a little but not enough to allow a person to get in. This also stops small children from falling out. Keep the keys to your window locks out of sight and safe from anyone opening the window without permission.

Casement windows

There are locking devices that work in a similar way to the sash window lock. They work like a door chain, but as there is no loose chain, the window will not be damaged. The product is non-handed and can be used for inward and outward opening windows.

There are many different solutions to locking windows. Some are suitable for both wood and UPVC. The most common is a standard window bolt. It is well worth the trouble, time and small investment to fit window locks.

Door bell vs door knocker

Consider both. A door knocker doesn't break down or need batteries, but if you live five storeys up, you may not hear it. Door knockers require drilling through the door and fixings tightened from the inside. If the door is hollow, fit an extra large washer to the inside of the door fixing. For some reason, folks love to use the knocker as a pull handle and may end up wrenching it from the door.

If there is a bell fitted that no longer works, remove it by prising off the cover to reveal one or two screws holding it on. This way, you will not incur the wrath of friends visiting for the first time who have been standing waiting for an answer that will never come. If you have a bell, use your initials rather than your first name to identify the bell as yours.

To save time and a lot of unsightly wiring, fit a wireless door bell, which consists of the bell push and the chimes, and can be fitted anywhere inside your home. Each half can be opened up and fitted using one or two screws. Ding dong!

Letter box security

Consider fitting a letter box cover if it is possible to insert a hand through your letter box from outside or if it's possible to see into your home. A cover will also deter key fishing – using a fishing rod to snag any keys lying around on hallway tables or stands. Attractive brass covers can be fitted to the inside of your door that allow the visor to open about a third of the way, so letters can get in but prying eyes can't. These will also keep out draughts.

SNUG AS A BUG – DRAUGHT-PROOFING YOUR HOME

Rattling sash windows and Arctic-style draughts blowing through the gaps sound familiar? One of the simplest ways to ensure your home is environmentally friendly and save yourself huge amounts on heating bills is to make sure your home is draught-proofed. This is especially true if you live in a period property.

Simple techniques can be used to reduce heat loss and your fuel costs. However, damming up all the gaps has its disadvantages too, as a house needs ventilation to get rid of moisture generated by steamy baths, cooking pots and even us.

If you feel cold air coming in, then warm air is certainly escaping – a simple way to check for draughts is to light a candle and move it around the frames of windows and doors. Where the flame flickers most is where you have a draught. Once you find it, you can then deal with it.

Draught-proofing doors and windows

DIFFICULTY RATING

What's a draught and what's ventilation?

Ventilation is good; it keeps the house fresh and healthy. The air inside your home needs to be replaced with air from outside so that it doesn't become stale and damp. Homes need to be fitted with vents in the right spaces – extractor fans above stoves and in bathrooms, as well as wall vents and trickle vents in modern window construction. Draughts, however, are caused by accidental gaps.

Some gaps can be filled safely, but care needs to be taken when treating rooms with open fires or open flues as it's important that these have good ventilation. Care is also needed in moisture-producing rooms such as bathrooms, kitchens and laundry rooms. A build up of condensation causes the dreaded DAMP!

TIME FRAME

An hour or so for each small project

YOU WILL NEED

Foam or rubber strips
Scissors
Damp cloth
Fine sanding paper
Brush strip
Hacksaw
Measuring tape
Pencil
File

There are several methods of draught-proofing doors and windows and one of the easiest methods uses self-adhesive foam strips purchased from most DIY stores. If you are installing these on doors and windows that open regularly, bear in mind the strips can wear quickly. Use self-adhesive rubber strips instead as these are more hard-wearing.

Make sure that there is enough clearance for the

Chimneys and fireplaces

If you don't use your fireplace, your chimney may be a big source of unnecessary draughts. You can board up the fireplace with a piece of MDF screwed or glued in place and then painted, or buy a chimney balloon – a sort of inflatable cushion that blocks up the chimney. Quick, easy and effective!

draught-proof strip by running a piece of card around the frame (or area that you are fitting the strips). If the card sticks in a certain area then you may not have enough clearance for the draught proofing; it also means that you are less likely to have a draught in this area. Make sure the surface you are sticking the strips to is clean so these adhere properly.

Brush strips are another great way to eliminate draughts and are effective in areas that move a lot such as front doors or letter boxes.

If you feel cold air around the frames of your doors and windows, the simplest and cheapest solution is to fit lengths of foam strip in the gaps. To reduce the

It's curtains for you!

A fun way of keeping the cold out is to put up some nice thick curtains – more exciting than self-adhesive foam strips, and you can change the look of a room with some really interesting fabrics. Think about switching curtains from summer to winter. In the winter you can have nice velvety drapes and switch to softer, flowing fabrics in the summer.

loss of heat from under the door, fit a double-sided draught excluder made from foam, which will allow the door to move but stop some of the heat escaping. The simplest just slide under the door but some need to be screwed onto the wood. You can use short screws for this as it does not require much strength.

There are two options if you have casement windows that open – foam/rubber tape or brush strip. Foam tape is an inexpensive solution and can be fitted without tools. Take care to use the correct depth of tape; too small and there will still be a draught but if it's too big the window won't close and could be damaged. The foam strip doesn't last very long and will have to be replaced every few years.

If using the tape method, make sure the surfaces are clean and dry. Wipe off any dust around the door or window frame and sand down any nibs in the paintwork that will prevent the tape from sticking. Use the draught tape to measure lengths as it isn't so important to be very accurate. Remove the glue paper from the tape slowly as you work from top to bottom of the door or window.

If using the brush strip method, measure the size of each section to be fitted with a strip. Cut with a hacksaw and file off burrs to make smooth.

Doors can be draught-proofed in the same way as windows but don't forget the keyhole and letterbox. You can fit a specially made metal cover to help with draughts. Remember to measure the letterbox before you buy a cover.

OTHER DRAUGHT-PROOFING POSSIBILITIES

Floorboards and skirtings

Masses of air circulates behind the walls of a house. This is especially true if you happen to live in a period house. You can block cracks in floorbords and skirting boards using flexible filler since these expand and contract with the seasons. Fillers block gaps permanently so be careful when you apply them and wipe off any excess or mess with a damp cloth before it dries. Fillers may break down over time, but can easily be reapplied.

Cellars and lofts

If you are lucky enough to have a cellar or loft, then an easy way to keep the draughts at bay is to board the ceiling of the cellar or the floor of the loft. Applying sheets of plasterboard is relatively easy as you just screw it into the wooden joists. Not only will this make your cellar or loft less draughty but it will make it a nicer environment to spend time in. If you do decide to do this, don't cover any pipework or cables without marking where they are on the plasterboard. This is also a great opportunity to get a proper light fitted, although this is a job for a professional.

SIZE DOESN'T MATTER – SMALL PROJECTS TO BOOST CONFIDENCE

It's understandable to be daunted by a kitchen refit, but a great way to feel your way into DIY is to tackle projects that don't require drilling deep holes into your walls. Here are a few suggestions to get you thinking. Adapt any idea to suit your own tastes and requirements.

SPACE SAVERS

Additions inside existing storage areas can double the amount of stuff you can stuff into them. It's a great way to gain confidence and you can close the door on any less-than-perfect results!

Shoe organizer and half-shelf

To turn a slim cupboard into a shoe organizer, place the shelves at an angle to hold the shoes in place. You can fit more shoes in this way.

Sometimes, just adding an extra half-shelf in a cupboard will be enough to double your storage. Melamine-coated particle board comes in many depths and is perfect for this add-on extra. Buy extra metal shelf supports and drill into your cabinet walls; insert the shelf supports and your new shelf.

ANTIQUE ANTICS

If you have furniture that has seen better days, there are several quick-fix solutions to bring it back to life. If you know a bit about revamping old furniture you can hunt for bargains in car-boot sales and charity shops and transform your home with one-off wonders. If you have a piece of old furniture that looks a bit shabby and you think it would be better suited to the dump, think again! (Especially in these days of the three Rs – reuse, recycle, revamp.) There are ways you can rescue said item. Anything can be painted, including melamine and laminate veneers (mainly the flat-pack stuff). The key to painting anything is ironically the 'key'. A key is a finely scratched surface to which paint or varnish will adhere. You need to make sure that you prepare the surface properly and use the correct paints.

Wooden furniture

Let's say you have an old pine chest of drawers. You can revamp wood by oiling it to give it a more matt and natural finish or paint it a pretty

HALF-SHELF TO MAXIMIZE STORAGE

Pull-out storage caddy

Screw casters on to a board and you have a contraption you can move around. You can use this principle to build a cube or a tower of open shelves to add extra storage inside a cupboard or make use of space under spare beds by creating bespoke storage boxes.

colour! To begin, you will need to prepare the surface: make sure the item is clean and dry and if it's been sitting around for a long time, clean it with some sugar soap solution to get rid of general grime and dirt (see 'Preparation – Decor Decorum' page 66).

Once it's dry, sand the surface to provide a key for the new finish. Use grade 120 or finer sandpaper and lightly sand all the surfaces in the direction of the grain and if there are any stubborn nicks or cracks, sand these with a finer grade of paper. Clean the surface using a tack cloth to wipe away all the small, barely visible motes of sanding dust. Tack cloths are special cloths you can buy that are slightly waxy and designed to pick up very fine sanding dust.

Remove any removable parts and handles, and if there are drawers take these out and work on them separately. If you are finding it difficult to take the handles off then cover them in masking tape so these don't get painted or varnished. This is also a great opportunity to replace the handles for something more personal – new handles can really jazz up an old item of furniture so get hunting in charity shops or online for something that fits the new style.

If you find any holes or cracks now is the time to fill them. If you are keeping the wood a natural colour by oiling or varnishing it, then choose a filler that is a similar colour to the finish you are aiming for. Coloured wood fillers are a bit more pricey but they are well worth the money if you are planning to keep wood natural – white filler would look truly horrible. Once the filler is dry, sand the area so that the filler is flat and seamlessly blends with the piece of furniture.

Oiling wooden furniture

Oiling provides a soft satin sheen to wood that is very durable. This treatment is only suitable for new wood or wood that has been stripped bare or previously oiled. If you have a varnished piece of wood then all the varnish will need to be removed before you can apply an oil coat. There are several types of oil available. Try boiled linseed oil for a rich deep finish or Danish oil for a lighter effect.

Apply oils with a lint-free cloth and add further layers after coats have dried to achieve your desired finish. This is a satisfying process as you are nurturing the wood and can get fantastic results. This finish is not resistant to water stains so to avoid white glass rings, use coasters or some protective surface on your revamped piece of furniture.

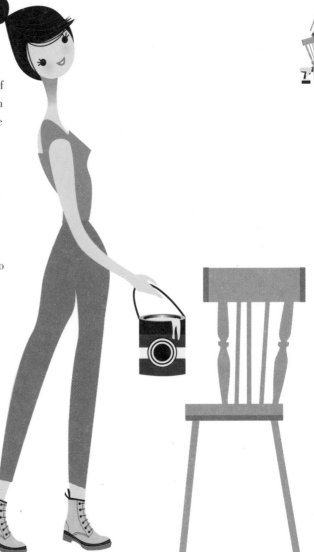

Trade secret

When using a claw hammer to remove picture hooks and nails, place a bit of cardboard between the wall and the claw of the hammer to prevent scuff marks.

Waxing furniture

Completely different from oils, wax provides a great finish to furniture and is easy to maintain. Waxed surfaces can be marked by heat and water and they can get dirty easily because the wax makes the surface slightly sticky. Therefore it is best to use waxes on items that are not used every day. It can be applied to new or newly stripped wood or to oiled surfaces. The most commonly used wax finish is beeswax, which varies in colour – bleached and white varieties are also available. Carnuba wax is often added to beeswax to reduce its slight tackiness and improve its durability. Paraffin wax is a soft wax, mainly used in less expensive polishes. This is sometimes added to high-quality wax polishes to make them softer and easier to apply.

Painting furniture

A lick of paint can make a huge difference to a shappy old piece of furniture – to paint wooden furniture follow all the preparation steps above. Once the item is prepared, apply a primer to the wood and then a top coat. Depending on the colour, you might need to apply two coats. If you want to create a distressed look, once a the top coat is dry, roughly sand the piece and then apply a lighter colour of paint to the item, but water this down so it's a bit thinner and also lighter in colour.

If you want to paint melamine furniture, you will need to sand the item well to create a good key for the paint. Also the piece of furniture will need to be primed properly and you will need a very robust paint such as an epoxy or oil-based paint to cover the surface. You may need to source these from specialist paint stores; ask your local paint store what is best for your particular item. Spray paints can also work well for these types of surfaces.

Furniture reviving polish

Old, dingy and dusty wooden furniture can be treated with a traditional furniture reviver mix made like a salad dressing in an old bottle. The theory behind the ingredients is that the vinegar cuts through the dirt on the furniture, the turpentine slightly dissolves the old wax polish build-up without stripping and removing the patina of age and the boiled linseed oil feeds and nourishes the wood. Buy linseed oil and the turpentine from a good hardware store and the vinegar from the supermarket. Use white distilled vinegar rather than the aged balsamic (you aren't making a salad, after all)!

YOU WILL NEED

⅓ part boiled linseed oil
⅓ part turpentine
⅓ part white distilled vinegar
Empty bottle
Old toothbrush
Soft cloths

Shake the mixture in the bottle until it emulsifies, just like making salad dressing. It will smell a bit like an antique shop.

Before you launch into reviving your piece of furniture, test the mixture first. Pour a little mixture on a soft cloth and test the result on a hidden area of the furniture. This works well on neglected, thirsty wood, but it can be too harsh for finely finished pieces. Rub the surface in small circles and see if the dirt/old wax comes off on the cloth. Leave the area to dry for 24 hours and then buff to a shiny finish. (If the surface has gone cloudy or has become sticky then don't use the mixture on the rest of the piece.) Use an old toothbrush dipped in the mixture to clean fiddly bits of moulding that have filled with dust. Protect the surrounding area with dust sheets as the brushing may cause splatters.

If the finish on the piece is beyond hope and it isn't *Antiques Roadshow*-worthy, a coat of paint in the same shade as the wall will help it blend into the background while retaining its usefulness.

DECOR DECORUM – PAINTING AND WALLPAPERING PROJECTS

Okay, now the fun begins and you can really get to grips with your DIY mania. Changing the decor in a room has to be one of the most satisfying ways to make a real difference to your home. In the following pages we cover DIY painting and decorating, including how to prepare surfaces, fill cracks and holes and select paint and paper.

Once you've assembled all your tools, equipment and materials, you can begin. We have outlined the order of work for painting ceilings, walls and woodwork, as well as how to tackle that tricky panelled door and sash window. There are also detailed instructions on how to wallpaper; where to begin and how to match tricky patterns.

Painting a room

Of all the projects possible, the most gratifying is to decorate a room. Fresh paint and clean walls lift the spirits and welcome friends and family. If you are starting over again, decorating gives you a chance to cover those memories and move on. The energy produced while carrying out the task produces endorphins and lifts depression so happiness isn't JUST in the choice of paint colour or wallpaper.

If you are nervous about colour keep to pale ivories and warm shades of cream. White is great if you like an 'art gallery' feel but it can seem cold and heartless in a way that warm off-whites don't. You can paint the walls the same colour as the woodwork to maximize the illusion of spaciousness. Bold colours used just on woodwork allow you to be brave without going overboard.

If you are feeling more adventurous and know what colours you love, exercise a little restraint and paint bold colours on one wall at a time. They will look lightest and brightest on a wall opposite the window and often one wall is enough. Paint a wall the same colour as the sofa for a confident complement.

TIME FRAME

3–4 days depending on scope of project

YOU WILL NEED

Sandpaper
Sanding block/sander
Drop cloths
Step ladder
50 mm (2 inch) paint brush
Roller and tray
Radiator roller if you have tight places to paint
Rags to wipe up splashes
White spirit (cleaning brushes and rollers)

The time required to complete a painting project is a moveable feast and will depend on the amount of time you spend preparing (sometimes the most time-consuming part). Sanding a skirting board to a mirror finish might not be worth it if it will be hidden by a sofa all its life. However, having to stare at a bump on the wall by the TV every night can be avoided if you spend a little more time sanding before painting.

What colour?

Start by looking at paint swatches on a card. As the perception of colour changes depending on the colour next to it, take several cards of each colour, cut them out and join the swatches to make a bigger swatch. Now move it around the room and see how it looks on all the walls. The colour will look different on the wall by the window compared with the wall on which the sun shines. If you can, buy a small tester pot and apply the paint to the wall. Remember to test

it on several walls in the same room and take into account the effect of the colour beneath it.

Where to start

Empty the room. If this isn't possible then move out what you can and cover the remaining furniture with plastic dust sheets and newspaper. Move as much stuff into the centre of the room so you have easy access to the walls. Use masking tape to protect areas you don't want painted but remember to remove the tape as soon as possible because it gets difficult to remove if left too long.

Filling holes and cracks

Fill small holes where a wall fixing or picture hook has been removed by pressing filler into the hole with a **spatula** or **filler knife**. Wait until it is dry and sand lightly using a sandpaper block to achieve a flat surface. Picture hooks can be removed with a claw hammer; for stubborn ones, try a tap with a screwdriver in between the wall and the hook for a bit of friendly persuasion. If the wall fixings are in hollow walls, leave them be. You might end up removing more of the wall than you want. Take a hammer and a nail set and gently tap them just below the surface. Now you can skim

them over with wall filler and a filler knife. If the hole is about the size of a fist or a foot, pick away any loose plaster and pour some wood glue on an old newspaper and scrunch it into the hole. Wait for it to dry and then fill the hole with filler. This way, the filler won't just fall into the cavity.

If plaster is basically sound, fill with white powder filler or ready-mixed filler. If plaster is loose and crumbly, you may need to cut out and replaster.

1. After clearing crack of dust and debris, use a scrap of wood to mix filler by adding water.

2. With the loaded filler knife, apply the filler across the crack and press in well.

3. Apply filler in the opposite direction and smooth off any excess. Leave to dry.

4. Wipe excess from the filler knife against the board and wash clean before filler sets.

Preparing the surfaces

Wash all the woodwork. Use sugar soap to remove grease and then rinse to remove the sugar soap. Sugar soap is a cleaning material, commonly composed of sodium carbonate, sodium phosphate and sometimes sodium silicate as an abrasive. Other chemicals might be added to modify the performance or preserve the product. The dry powder looks like table sugar, hence the name. Wear gloves as it is a strong alkaline and will sting.

Lightly sand all woodwork to provide a 'key', a finely scratched surface that will hold the paint well. Scars left by removed pictures, scuffs from suitcases and furniture and accidental damage are hard to live with. Removing the signs of past lives can be very cathartic and is easy to do.

Sand woodwork following the grain of the wood to provide a key for fresh paint.

Get rid of old grease stains from blue poster putty by rolling a ball of white bread over the mark. Stubborn stains may need a tiny dab of dry-cleaning fluid. To remove old stickers, use a non-toxic adhesive remover poured on a rag.

Water stains on walls and ceilings from overflowing baths or burst pipes have long memories and if you paint over them with ordinary paint they will reappear again and again. 'Die' you say, 'die', but they don't. A small can of stain block will go a long way and only needs to be painted over the offending streaks. Wait until it dries and then paint over the water block patch with the desired paint.

Murals and stickers

A fabulously easy way to make a quirky and individual design statement is to apply ready-made mural stickers to create maximum 'wow' factor. If you are feeling adventurous, paint your own mural using sample pots of paint. The sky is the limit.

Old wallpaper

If you are planning to paint over wallpaper ensure that it is securely stuck to the wall, otherwise strip it off. Heavy patterns may show through paint so try a test patch first. Red ink often comes through a covering layer of paint, but if you paint over the red bits with silver paint (I know it's odd but it acts as a barrier) then the red won't show through.

Porous/flaky surfaces

Clean down and paint porous or flaky surfaces with a sealer or primer paint. PVA glue thinned with water can be used as a sealer coat.

Black mould

Treat this problem with a fungicidal wash and remember to find the cause and cure it (condensation or damp walls) before you paint, otherwise you will simply be postponing the problem and the mould will return. After the wash, use a fungicidal paint.

Fittings

Remove or loosen light fittings and fixtures and protect with masking tape and/or plastic bags. Remember to switch off the electrical source when unscrewing sockets, switch covers and ceiling roses.

Cover light fixtures with old plastic bags or newspaper to avoid that speckled look!

Paint coverage per litre/quart

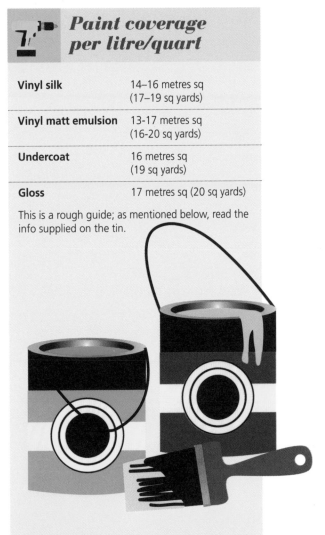

Vinyl silk	14–16 metres sq (17–19 sq yards)
Vinyl matt emulsion	13-17 metres sq (16-20 sq yards)
Undercoat	16 metres sq (19 sq yards)
Gloss	17 metres sq (20 sq yards)

This is a rough guide; as mentioned below, read the info supplied on the tin.

How much paint?

Measure the area you wish to paint and use the information above and on the paint tin to calculate how much paint to buy. Remember to subtract the areas of the doors and windows. When buying paint, read the tin label. It will tell you how many square metres/yards can be covered. But keep in mind that this can only be a guide as more paint will be required if changing a Goth cave into an angel haven.

Painting tools and equipment

FITCH   13 MM (5 IN) BRUSH   38 MM (1½ IN) BRUSH   68 MM (2½ IN) BRUSH   PAINT KETTLE   PAINT SHIELD   MASKING TAPE

STIRRING STICK   DUST SHEETS   WHITE SPIRITS   RAG   SMALL FOAM RUBBER ROLLER AND TRAY   LARGE OR MEDIUM PILE ROLLER AND TRAY

ROLLER EXTENTION HANDLE

PAINT PADS   PAINT LOADING TROUGH (FOR PAINT PADS)   178 MM (7 IN) FLAT BRUSH

ORDER OF WORK

Paint downwards. If you are painting the ceiling as well as the walls, start with that. It's also good to know that it's the hardest and most back-breaking task of all. Wipe off any spills or drips on the walls as you go – it's easier to wipe off wet paint than sand off dry paint. Don't be discouraged by the strain, the rest of the room will be plain sailing by comparison.

Matt or silk?

The choice is all yours. Matt paint has no shine and helps hide defects if you have a lumpy uneven wall. Silk/satin has a slight sheen and is great for reflecting a little more light. Gloss is a choice for metal or woodwork – it is really shiny and will need to be applied with care as every sag will show.

Getting started

If the new colour is very different from the old one, apply the first coat thinned with water as an undercoat, using about 1 part water to 8 parts paint. Check that the brand of paint CAN be diluted with water. Be careful when using more than one tin of specially mixed paint as there can be colour differences. To ensure an even colour, mix them together in a plastic bucket and stir well before painting.

Painting the ceiling

Flat paint is the traditional choice for ceilings as it hides lumps and bumps, but if you have a good finish on your ceiling, then why not try a sheen? It bounces light off and makes the room brighter.

First paint around the edges of the cornices and edge of the ceiling with a well-filled brush that has been gently wiped against the side of the tin. Feather out paint at the edges. Pour paint from your tin into a paint tray to about a third full. Dip in the roller and work paint into the fleece of the roller by rolling against the slope on the tray. This 'charges' the roller.

Working from a window side of the room, paint the ceiling in a series of cross hatch strokes. Reload the roller as it becomes dry and maintain a single coat as you paint. Finish off each section of paint by lightly rollering over in one direction to even out the paint (this is known as laying off).

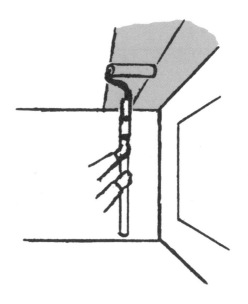

Use an extension pole to roller the ceiling. It's quicker and easier than constantly moving a ladder. Work in manageable strips.

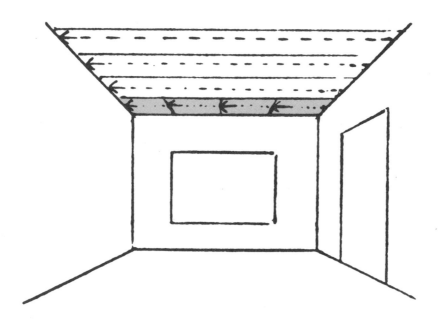

Start painting the ceiling with a roller from the window side of the room and work towards the back of the room. Work in strips and finish one before you move to the next.

Walls

First paint the corners and edges of walls with a smallish brush, feathering out the paint as you go. When using the roller work from the top of a wall to the bottom in bands of cross hatching patches. Allow each coat to dry for 4 hours minimum before applying the next coat.

✔ WORK ON! Never leave a wall or ceiling half done as you will always notice the join.

✔ WASH UP. Wash the roller straight away with lots of water (if using a water-soluable paint). One method of cleaning the fleece is to use a paint scraper to squeeze all the paint off under running water. If you are taking a short break in between walls, put the roller and tray into a plastic bag and seal it. This way it won't develop a crust. Wipe away any paint drips straight away with a damp cloth, so they don't harden.

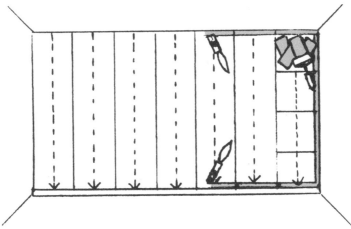

Start to paint the walls of the room by 'cutting in' – using a small brush to paint all the tricky edges around the ceilings, skirtings, windows and door before you start to roller. When rollering work in a series of cross-hatched patches (see right-hand corner of drawing).

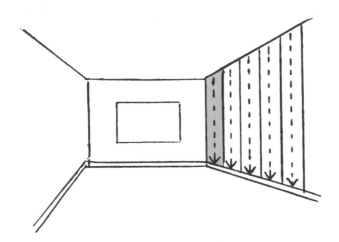

Starting from the window side (the light source) of the room, apply paint with a roller in wide strips using the cross-hatching action.

Work from the top of the wall to bottom and finish that strip before you start rollering and cross-hatching the next one.

Painting a room – woodwork, windows and doors

Gloss or semi-matt are the paints of choice for these surfaces, and like the previous project this one requires similar levels of preparation before you can launch in.

YOU WILL NEED

Dust sheets
Set of appropriate brushes
White spirit/brush cleaner
Jam jars for cleaning brushes
Step ladder
Old newspapers and rags for spills
Stir sticks
Screwdriver to remove the paint pot lid
Enough paint for the job

Preparation

If painting new wood, sandpaper it till smooth. Paint knots with a special sealant – if you don't, the resin will continue to seep through the paint leaving ring marks. Apply a primer coat and allow to it dry for at least 12 hours.

If painting over already-painted wood, wash down the surface with sugar soap and water. If the previous paint is oil-based, then sand down lightly with fine sandpaper to remove any paint lumps and bumps and provide a key. Apply wood primer to any bare spots and remove any cracked or peeling areas with a paint scraper and fill with fine filler. Fill cracks and

Applying paint

1. Start to apply paint in overlapping, criss-cross brush strokes.

2. Then brush the paint out in horizontal cross strokes.

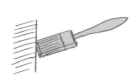

3. Now change direction and brush paint out in vertical strokes, finishing on an up stroke.

4. For undercoat use only the tips of the bristles during the final laying off.

5. For gloss paint, use only the sides of the bristles during the final laying off.

6. Lift the brush off the surface as you come to the end of the laying-off stroke.

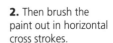

Trade secret

For a good paint finish, only dip your brush into the paint to halfway up the bristles. Gently wipe the brush against the inside lip of the tin or paint jar to remove any excess paint. This prevents overloading the brush and avoids runs down half your wall and your arm. Not such a good look!

small holes with filler. Remove any handles and fittings from doors and windows if possible and apply masking tape over the closing mechanism so that you don't shut yourself in a room without a handle on the door.

Starting to paint

Decant paint into a sturdy pot to avoid carrying a heavy paint tin around with you. Wipe the rim of the large paint tin and firmly replace the lid to ensure you don't kick it over and say bad words.

Paint your prepared surfaces with undercoat to suit the top coat. Apply thinly and allow the undercoat to

These are slightly more complicated to paint so plan ahead if you are tackling a sash window. Paint on a fine day in the morning and if you have to close the windows before the paint is dry, put a matchstick in between the sashes and frame to keep them from drying stuck together.

Before starting, make sure the window will still close after an extra layer of paint is applied. Insert a postcard between the window and frame. If you can't do this then you will have to sand or use a heat gun to remove the extra paint layer. Paint in the order shown in the illustration below.

Painting a panelled door requires a similar treatment. This minimizes the look of 'joined' paint caused by applying fresh paint next to a drying surface. Paint in the order shown in the illustration opposite.

1. Move lower sash up and top sash down, then paint bottom section of top sash and bottom section of lower sash. Next paint all the exposed runner sides.

2. Now move the top sash towards top, lower sash to bottom. Paint the rest of the top sash and the exposed top runner tracks (see shaded area).

3. Finally, paint the lower sash, including the top edge, as well as the surrounding mouldings, the tracks and the window sill. Leave to dry.

dry for 24 hours. Apply the top coat evenly. Do not overload the brush or the paint will run. It's a good idea to use new brushes for the undercoat as it will help to get rid of any loose bristles.

Use a series of cross strokes in flat areas, brushing and smoothing out across the panel. Complete a section at a time or finish the whole area. On panels, work from the edges in towards the middle. Brush over drips or runs as they happen. Do not allow them to harden. If they DO harden, let them dry, sand down and repaint the area.

For panel doors, decide what colour you want to paint the edges – normally it's the same as the inside of the frame. For flush doors, paint the edges first, then paint a series of square areas down the door, paint each square up and down, then sideways. Finish off with light vertical strokes towards the finished area. Work on the next section straight away and don't stop.

For windows, paint the glazing bars with an angled brush. Paint the edges close to the glass first, then finish off with even strokes across the bar.

Painting a panelled door

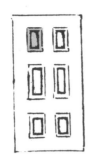

1. Start by wedging the door open, then paint the edge of the door.

2. Next paint the mouldings and panel. Continue to paint all the other panels.

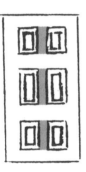

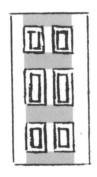

3. Now paint the vertical centre rails between the panels.

4. Then paint the horizontal cross rails between the panels.

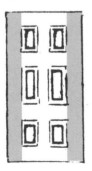

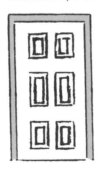

5. Paint the two outer vertical areas (called styles).

6. Finally, paint the surrounding door frame.

Cleaning and storing brushes

After use, squeeze any remaining paint off the brush against the edge of the tin, then use an old rag or newspaper to clean any excess paint from the ferrule and handle. Pour 8 cm (3 in) of brush cleaner or white spirit into a jar and mash the brush gently against the bottom of the jar to open the bristles and allow the solvent to work its way into the middle of the brush. Remove as much paint as you can in this way. Now place the brush in an empty sink and pour washing-up liquid over the bristles. Work the suds into the bristles with your fingers (use rubber gloves). When the white spirit and the washing-up liquid have emulsified, rinse well under warm running water. Don't forget to gently open the middle of the brush and get at the roots. If there is still paint on the brush, pour new white spirit into the jar and repeat the process. Leave to dry in the air so the bristles will keep their shape.

Trade secret

If you have to take a short break for a much-needed sit-down with a nice cup of tea and biscuit, for instance, cover your paint tray, brush or roller in clingfilm to prevent it drying out.

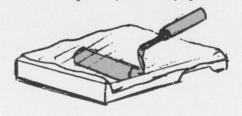

Wallpapering a room

YOU WILL NEED

Pasting table
Utility knife and long scissors
Paper hanging brush
Paste
Plastic buckets for paste and water
Stirring sticks
Spirit level
Big sponge (a clean car wash one is fine)
Clean damp cloths for wiping excess paste
Wallpaper
Tape measure or folding rule

Preparation

For all DIY projects, the end results often depend on the amount of effort that goes into preparation before you actually get to the good part – which in this case is papering a room with lovely wallpaper. What preparation you do before wallpapering depends on the surface of your walls.
✔ Painted plaster. Wash down the walls and use a scraper to get rid of any flaky paint. Fill

Wallpapering tools and equipment

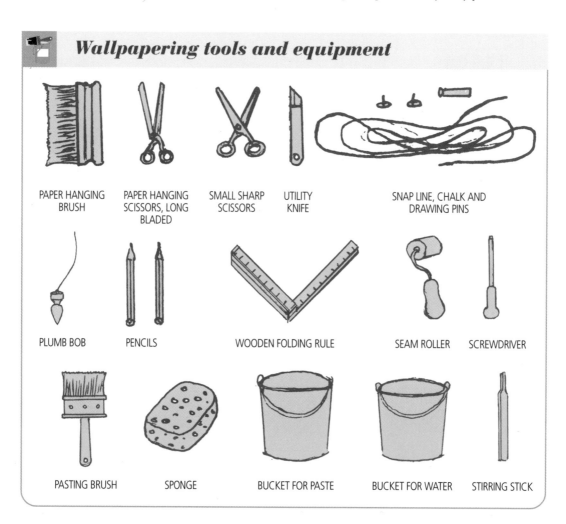

PAPER HANGING BRUSH

PAPER HANGING SCISSORS, LONG BLADED

SMALL SHARP SCISSORS

UTILITY KNIFE

SNAP LINE, CHALK AND DRAWING PINS

PLUMB BOB

PENCILS

WOODEN FOLDING RULE

SEAM ROLLER

SCREWDRIVER

PASTING BRUSH

SPONGE

BUCKET FOR PASTE

BUCKET FOR WATER

STIRRING STICK

cracks and holes with filler. Seal the surface of the wall with watered-down white glue or wallpaper paste. Apply lining paper first if the wall surface is very uneven.

✔ Fresh plaster. Paint with water-based paint and leave to dry. Allow two weeks for lightweight plaster to dry and up to six weeks for sand and cement to dry before papering.

✔ Plasterboard. If unpainted then paint with a sealer and apply lining paper.

✔ Old wallpaper. It's a really good idea to strip off old wallpaper using a **steam stripper** (see right), and scraping it off with a stripping knife. Use the steamer in sections of about a metre (a yard) at a time so it doesn't dry out. Score the wallpaper carefully so you don't damage the surface of the plaster underneath. This will help the steam get behind the paper, making it easier to scrap it off. Don't use too much steam or it will seep into the plaster permanently.

✔ Skirting boards. Use decorators' caulk to fill the gaps in between the wall and the skirting boards so that you can achieve a neat finish.

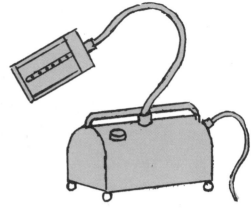

STEAM WALLPAPER STRIPPER

Where to begin

Start from a window. Measure away from the window one roll width less 25 mm (5 inches) and mark a vertical line using a spirit level and a pencil (see the illustration below). Hang the first length with one edge against the vertical line, with the other side trimmed around the window. Work away from the window and around the room, finishing in a corner. Paper the chimney breast and feature walls from the centre outwards.

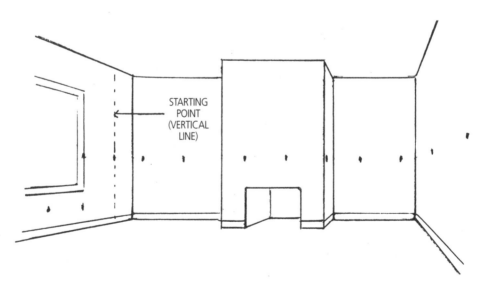

STARTING POINT (VERTICAL LINE)

Use a spirit level and plumb line to create a straight vertical line on your wall. This will be the starting point for your first drop. Then using a roll of wallpaper as a measuring guide, mark the wallpaper widths all around the room in order to see how the joins will work. You don't want to be joining paper on an outside corner, so make adjustments.

How much wallpaper do you need?

Wallpaper comes in rolls of about 10 metres (33 feet) long by 53 cm (20 in) wide. Measure the height of walls (add 150 mm/6 inches for trimming). Measure the total length and subtract areas of window and doors to give the total area of wallpaper required. A standard roll covers about 5 metres sq (54 sq ft) so divide the total wallpaper area by 5 to give you the number of rolls required. For the lovely huge patterns, add 10 percent to the number of rolls to allow for wastage in matching up patterns. You can roughly mark on your walls to help you measure up if need be, using the height of room and width of roll. To calculate for the ceiling, measure the width of room and see how many lengths you can get from the roll at the room width, then mark out how many pape widths you can get into the length of the room.

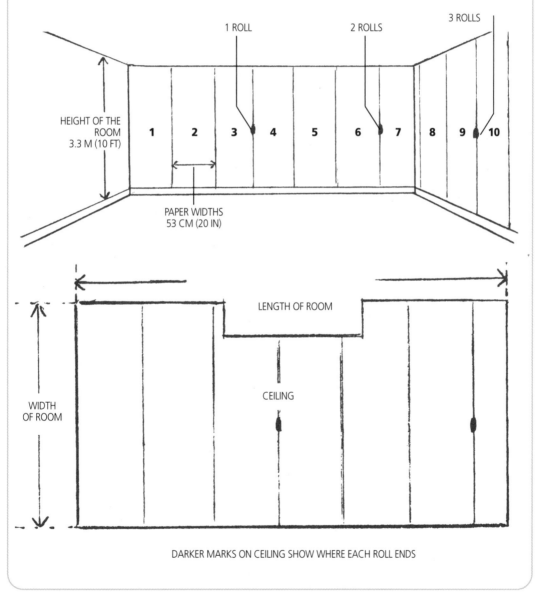

DARKER MARKS ON CEILING SHOW WHERE EACH ROLL ENDS

Measure the centre point and then divide the roll width so that there is a drop in the centre.

Cutting and pasting

Follow the instructions on the pack and mix up the paste in a bucket. Make sure it's not too sloppy. Cut two lengths to get the hang of it. Add at least 150 mm (6 inches) plus the length of the repeat if your paper has a large pattern (information will be on the roll). Resist the temptation to cut all the lengths until you are confident of your measurements. Once you have pasted a length of paper (see below) let the paper sit

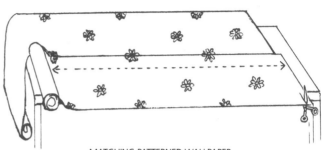

MATCHING PATTERNED WALLPAPER

for a few minutes so that it slightly absorbs the paste. This will allow the paper to settle tightly on the wall as it drys. When you get into your stride you can paste one drop ahead so there is always a

Pasting and folding wallpaper

Lay the paper on the table with one end at the top and brush the paste from the centre outwards, and towards the top. Fold over the top so the paste sticks

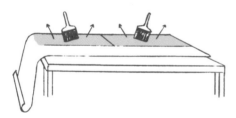

1. With one end of the paper near the end of the table, apply paste by brushing up and outwards.

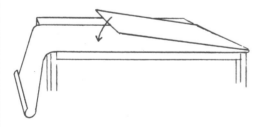

2. Fold over the pasted half onto itself so the pasted surfaces stick together.

together and move the paper up the table. Paste the other side and fold over that half, then allow the paper to sit.

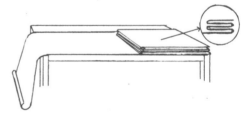

3. If your lengths are very long you may have to concertina-fold the length.

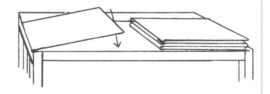

4. Now paste the second half and fold that half over on itself. Allow the length to rest for a few minutes.

rested drop ready to hang. Place the scissors and a large clean dry brush near your work area – either up the ladder or in your apron pocket.

✔ Drop one. Hang the pasted wallpaper over your arm and climb the ladder. Unfold one end and place the top against the wall with 75 mm (3 inches) to spare (see box right for step by steps). Make sure the edge is against the marked vertical line. If it isn't lined up, gently lift away from the wall and reposition. Gently brush the paper down from the centre of the roll, releasing the lower portion when the paper is in position.

Brush the paper into the top of the wall marking a crease very gently with the back of the scissors. Do the same with the skirting boards. Lift top and bottom away from wall and cut with scissors and brush back again. Be careful to wipe any excess paste from the ceiling and skirting before it dries.

✔ Drop two. After pasting and resting the next drop, slide the wallpaper into place next to drop one to make a neat butt joint. Wipe the joins gently to remove spare paste. Carry on around the room and end at a corner.

Hang ups

Take the pasted roll to the wall and slide into place. Use a clean brush to push the paper onto the wall; wipe off extra paste that squeezes out the sides.

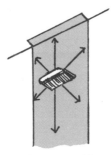 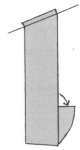

1. Leaving an extra bit at the top, position your first drop and brush into place.

2. Keep the folds together and extend one fold at a time.

3. With the back of scissors score a line, then lift paper and cut off the excess.

4. Dry-brush paper over the full length and make sure the paper is sitting nicely against the wall.

 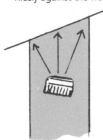

5. Scribe the top, cutting away surplus paper, then wipe away excess paste on ceiling.

6. Brush the paper into place at the top, brushing from the centre of the paper outwards.

Corners Don't be tempted to take a full roll round the corner; it will crease or create a void. Trim the paper to about 25 mm (1 inch) wide after the corner and overlap with the next sheet. Do this by gently turning the paper around the corners with your fingers, starting from the middle up to the ceiling and then down to the skirting boards.

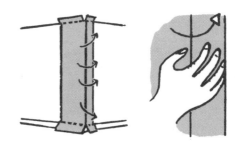

Windows and doors Put the pasted length on the door and brush onto the wall. Feel for the corner of the door frame and make a diagonal cut. Fold back the two flaps of paper loosely over the frame and gently score the fold line with the back of the scissors. Pull the paper away and cut along the crease.

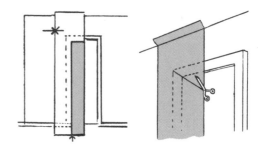

Light switches and fittings. Hang the paper over the switch and make a diagonal cut with a utility knife to the corners of the plate. Fold back, crease around the switch and cut a little inside the line. If the switch plate has been loosened, use a plastic blade to coax the paper behind the plate. For a pendant light (opposite) brush the paper up to the centre of the light. Make a hole in the paper with the point of your scissors, near the centre of the fitting, then make three more cuts from the centre hole to make a star burst shape. Scribe close to the fitting, continue pasting the length of paper across the ceiling, then go back and cut off the points at the scribed lines; brush snugly against the fitting.

Air bubbles If you find air bubbles, make a small cut into the wallpaper to release the air, then smooth back with a brush.

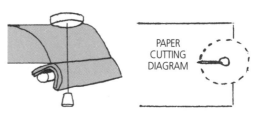

PAPER CUTTING DIAGRAM

1. Paste paper up to the fixture, make a cut in paper and proceed to make star burst cuts.

2. Scribe, continue to paper. Trim points snugly against fitting and secure in place.

LIGHT IT UP

The lighting in a room can have a dramatic effect on your mood. A new shade on an old lamp can really lift the decor of a room.Bare light bulbs from ceiling pendants cast harsh shadows and show up every defect in the room. They also remind you every time you switch on the light that the room is incomplete. Dirty, broken and uncoordinated shades on ceilings and lamps are very easy to remove and replace.

YOU WILL NEED

Step ladder
New shade
Screwdriver

Choose daytime for this task and always make sure the switch is off. You normally don't need to switch off the power to replace a simple shade. If you are using a step ladder, always make sure it is fully extended and firmly placed on the ground. If you are using a dining chair, test that it is stable by standing on it with shoes off. Place your feet over the legs if possible and don't use a folding chair as any foot movement may knock you off balance. If you feel uneasy about heights, place two chairs together and use a broom as an extra support.

Removing the old lampshade

First remove the light bulb. Light bulbs have either screw-in or bayonet connections. If you have never removed a light bulb before, you can practise on a table lamp before setting off up the ladder. Remember to tackle this when the bulb is cold, otherwise you're in for a nasty burn.

It helps to know how a ceiling light fitting is constructed. If a shade has been on for a long while, the plastic parts may have become brittle and may be difficult to unscrew. Turn off the power and spray a little WD-40 onto the part of the socket where the old shade is held in place. Wrapping a red rubber band around it helps with friction to remove it.

Paper lampshades

These design classics cost very little, can be bought in a range of shapes and sizes and are easy to install. Choose a white shade for maximum brightness. They often attach above the light fitting to the wire so don't require any unscrewing. Other fresh and bright lampshades cost very little and are available in many department stores. Remember that big and bold gives the impression of a confident space – smaller lampshades are best for side lights.

ON THE TILES – REMOVING, CHOOSING AND LAYING TILES

The beauty of tiles is that there is a fabulous array of choice. Tiles add colour, life and depth to any surface and if you are looking to revamp a room, tiles are a super option. The knack to tiling well is to choose the appropriate tiles for the job and also to take your time – like all DIY projects patience and planning are the keys to a good finish. As tiles are waterproof and easy to keep clean, they are great in kitchens and bathrooms. However, a certain amount of maintenance is needed, especially in high water areas – the grout between the tiles can discolour and attract mould. As tiles are rigid objects, consider well before laying them on a springy wooden floor; laying cork tiles or perhaps flexible vinyl tiles might be a better alternative.

TYPES OF TILES

Ceramic tiles are hard-wearing, easier to install and maintain than more complex materials such as glass or natural stone. Ceramic tiles can be glazed or painted so the range is vast. They can be used on floors and walls and are lighter than some natural stone tiles, therefore are great on plasterboard surfaces.

Natural stone tiles are beautiful but are not as uniform as ceramics in colour and shade. They take longer to fit than ceramic and some are very hard and difficult to cut. Some stone tiles, especially when polished, can be slippery when wet so be careful if using on floors. Some natural stones absorb anything that is spilled on them so be wary when choosing a stone for the kitchen, for instance. There are special aftercare products that will help to seal out unwanted moisture. This seals the tile and the same process will have to be repeated every year to keep the durability. Limestone, granite, marble, slate and travertine are all materials used to make tiles, each with their own plus and minus points.

 ## Tile finishes

Polished Ground and polished to a sheen or highly reflective (and slippery) surface

Antiqued Toned down with stains to give that 'lived-in' feel

Tumbled Softened at the edges

Glass tiles are really amazing to look at and come in a super range of fun colours. However, they can be extremely difficult to fit as they break into shards when cut. Also they are not recommended for flooring due to their slippery nature.

Mosaic tiles can be made from glass, ceramic or natural stone. They are laid on a mesh backing, which makes them easier to cut and fit. They are great for borders or to bring in a splash of colour if you choose predominantly neutral tiles elsewhere. These can be used on walls, floors, kitchens, bathrooms and are available in a vast range.

REMOVING OLD TILES

YOU WILL NEED

Cold chisel
Hammer
Goggles
Work gloves
Protective drop cloths
Heavyweight rubbish sacks

This is when you find out just how much adhesive was used to hold your old tiles on the wall. Lay protective drop cloths over the floor and nearby areas, since the edges of tiles could scratch or damage floors and porcelain as they fall. Wear your protective goggles. Starting at an edge or corner, place the cold chisel's tip in between the edge of tile and the wall. Hit the other end with the hammer. Do it cautiously until you get the hang of using the chisel.

As tiles break away, move the chisel towards the next exposed area and work from left to right (if you are right-handed) if possible and from top to bottom.

As broken tiles gather, place them in a sturdy rubble bag with strong handles for removal. Continue to use the chisel and hammer to remove excess adhesive still on the wall, taking care not to damage the surface underneath.

Trade secret

Think ahead and place the empty rubble bag close to a point of removal i.e. by the front or back door and transfer tiles to it. Don't fill it so full that you can't lift it to take it away.

Tiling an area

YOU WILL NEED

Tile spacers
Trowel or serrated spatula to spread adhesive
Adhesive
Grout
Grout float or spatula
Tile cutters
Nibblers
Hammer
Spirit level
Screwdriver and screws
Wooden battens
Pencil or china marker
Goggles
Sponge and cloth
Tiles
Barrier cream (this is dry dusty
work so use this on your hands)

Select a fairly slow-drying **adhesive** if it's the first time you have laid tiles. This will be forgiving if you have to remove a couple to readjust the spacing as you go along. If you buy super-fast drying adhesive the tiles will be very difficult to remove if you make a mistake.

When choosing **tile spacers**, the size will depend on how thick you want your grout lines. Remember the grout lines need to be in proportion to the size of tile. Don't have large lines on a small tile – it will look odd... unless that's your style.

Grout – powdered is better as you can mix up the consistency and amount you require, but ready-mixed is fine for small areas.

Planning ahead – before you even cut a tile!

Remember that you will need to leave the adhesive to dry for 24 hours before grouting and then the grout will need to be left for at least 12 hours before it's dry. So bear this in mind especially when doing a shower or bath area as you won't be

How many tiles?

To calculate how many tiles you need, measure the length of the area by the height if it's a wall or by the width if it's a floor or counter) and multiply the two figures together. This will give you the square area. Always buy 10 per cent extra to allow for breakage and wastage of the tiles as you cut. Then measure and calculate again. Remember, measure twice and you won't be crying that you haven't got enough tiles now that the sale is over.

able to use the area for two days. The same goes for tiled floors – tile your way out of the room so you don't get stuck in there for 24 hours and don't walk on the floor until the adhesive is dry!

Think it through

Planning is the most important part of tiling as the first tile laid will determine the end result. If you can, put a plan on paper so that you have laid out each tile before you cut anything or put anything on the wall. The ideal is to have equal-sized tiles at each end of the room (top, bottom and sides). This will make the tiling look symmetrical. When tiling a bathroom you need to think about where the fittings (shower, taps, shower screen etc.) are so that you can factor this into the plan and make sure this works with your tiling arrangement.

Preparing the surface

Once your old tiles are removed you will need to ensure that you have a smooth surface to tile on.

 ## Your first row of tiles

After you have secured your batten gauge to the wall, use the spreader to spread an even layer of adhesive on to the wall. Once you have covered a reasonable area, use the serrated edge to create horizontal lines in the adhesive.

Lay your first tile against the batten, using your pencil marks as a guide (see 'Preparing the surface' above for making and using a batten tile gauge). Press the tile firmly into place, then position the next tile against it using the tile spacers and your gauge as a guide.

Continue until you get to a point where you need to cut tiles. If any adhesive squeezes out onto the tiles make sure you wipe it off with the damp sponge before it dries. Normally, it's best to start at the bottom and work your way along and upwards as tiles will sit happily on the lower row. If your design makes this unfeasible, be extra careful to ensure that the tiles are firmly set in place.

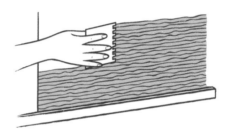

1. Apply adhesive to an area you can tile in about 15 minutes.

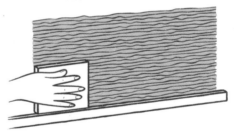

2. Apply tile and add firm pressure to remove air holes.

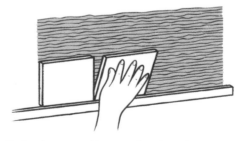

3. Continue to position your tiles along the tile gauge.

This may involved skimming the wall with plaster if the wall is in particularly bad condition or just filling holes where you can. Skimming is laying a thin coat of plaster on the surface – it's a skill you can acquire with much practice, but it may be more cost-effective to get an expert to do this – they can do it quicker and effortlessly. If you need to skim the walls, wait until the plaster is really dry so that no moisture gets trapped behind the tiles risking problems ranging from tiles falling off to mould growth.

You can use adhesive to level a wall to a certain extent but you don't want to rely solely on this method as little by little, any deviation from a flat surface may increase until you have a hill of tiling.

Before you begin, make a tile gauge by taking one of the battens and laying a row of tiles against it on the floor. Put spacers between the tiles and then use a pencil to mark where the tiles are on the batten

Trade secret

In a bathroom, leave a 3 mm (⅛ inch) gap at the bottom of tiles against a bath to allow for sealant. When tiling kitchen splashbacks, you will need to tile around sockets so make sure the electricity is switched off; wet hands and electricity don't make such good friends.

gauge stick. Use the gauge stick to help in layout and planning, and marking the wall where the bottom row of tiles will sit. Where possible, make sure this is a full tile and not a cut tile.

Screw the batten gauge stick to the bottom of your horizontal line and use the spirit level to make sure the guage is level.

Tile-cutting techniques

There are a number of ways to cut tiles and your choice of tile will help determine which method you use. Nibblers are particularly good for cutting finicky shapes to fit around piping and odd corners.

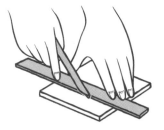

1. Run a tile cutter along a straight edge to score the surface of the

tile. Hold the tile over a small batten and snap along the line.

2. For a round cut, score tile then use a round-bladed tile cutter.

3. Use a nibbler for round and L-shaped cuts.

4. You can get ceramic cutting blades for some jigsaws.

How to mix grout

Place a small amount of powdered grout in a bucket and add water a little at a time, mixing together with a trowel until the grout is the consistency of cake mix. Don't mix too much grout at once otherwise it will set in the bucket, which is not only a waste of grout but also a waste of a good bucket!

Cutting tiles

Your choice of tile will help determine how you cut the tile. You can cut some tiles with a simple glass cutter, though this takes practice, so expect to lose a few tiles as you learn. Heavier tiles can be cut on **cutters** that work a bit like paper guillotines (see right). Material such as marble 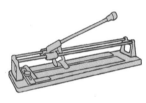 requires a wet cutting machine from a hire shop and is set up where it can make a mess and lots of noise. Don't be afraid of a wet wheel; they are easier to use than you think and make a job run smoothly and more quickly. For some, the grinding of the saw is too dentist-like to make this job a pleasure.

It is especially important to remember 'measure twice, cut once' while tiling, since mistakes can be expensive, especially when cutting natural stone. Offer the tile up to the wall and measure the area where the tile needs to fit. You can use a tile gauge if necessary but these are not essential. Mark a line on the tile showing the area to be cut and then extend the line using a spirit level or long straight edge. Remember to make allowance for grout lines. When you know the area to cut it's a good idea to hatch lines over the area to be discarded with a pencil so you know which part of the tile is going to

be used. This is especially important if you choose to make all your cuts first, then lay them later on.

If you have a very small amount to be removed from a tile, you will need to score a line where the cut is to be made with a glass/tile cutter and use a nibbler to remove the small flakes. Handle the nibbler like nail clipper and remove tiny areas first. Practise on a spare bit of tile before the stress of a real job.

Applying grout

Grout is the fine water-resistant seam between tiles. Once all your tiles have been laid you will need to leave them to dry for 24 hours before applying the grout. The adhesive needs to have air circulated behind it in order to set properly. When it comes to grouting, follow the manufacturers' instructions to mix grout. Apply grout using a grout float or spatula to spread the grout over the lines, pushing it into place to make sure you have a nice full line.

Use the spatula to spread grout between the tiles.

Sometimes, for corners and tight spaces you may be better off using your fingers to apply the grout like thin face cream – just make sure your fingers are clean. Use a damp sponge to gently clean away any excess grout, ensuring the grout line is not wiped away. Tidy up grout lines by running down the grout with a thin piece of dowel or round end of a pencil. When you have finished, clean the tiles by wiping with a damp cloth to polish off any grout and adhesive residue.

FEELING FLUSH – SIMPLE PLUMBING PROBLEMS SOLVED

For the most part plumbing is one of those specialist areas where it's sometimes easier to GSI (get someone in), in this case a trained plumber; however, there are a few things you can do on your own before resorting to the expense of a professional.

Unblocking a U-bend

YOU WILL NEED

Plunger
Vinegar
Baking soda
Bucket
Newspapers
Coathanger

If you have a blocked sink, you can try to fix it yourself before you call in a plumber. The first thing to try is a plunger on the sink drain – this creates a vacuum effect in the pipes and can shift a blockage in the pipes.

If this doesn't work you can buy expensive and environmentally harmful products that unclog sinks and drains, but you can make your own just as effectively with some vinegar and baking soda. Pour the bicarbonate of soda down the drain and try and make the drain as dry as possible. Then follow through with vinegar, and when it stops fizzing flush through with very hot water.

If your sink is still blocked then you may need to dismantle the U-bend, which isn't as scary as it sounds. The U-bend is the plastic or metal waste pipe under the sink. The nuts on each side of the U-bend should be hand tight so you shouldn't need tools for this job.

Place a washing-up bucket and some newspapers under the U-bend. Then unscrew each side of the U-bend being careful that the washers inside don't fall out. If you can, keep the U-bend upright and have a look inside the rims to see where the washers sit. The bucket is there for any residual water to drip into. Remove the washers from the U-bend and place to one side, then tip the U-bend into the bucket to clear the water. If you've managed to lose a piece of jewellery down the plughole, now is the time to rescue it!

Then unravel a wire coat hanger (or get some other poking device) and start clearing out the U-bend. Let's hope your precious ring is safe inside. Once you've cleared the blockage, take the U-bend to another sink to wash it through. You should also warn anyone else in the property not to use the sink while the U-bend isn't there.

When clean and the blockage has been removed, then reattach, making sure the washers are safely back in place. Screw the nuts so they are hand-tight; don't use tools as you can crack the plastic. Run warm water through the sink and check for leaks.

Plumbing in washing machine/dishwasher

DIFFICULTY RATING

YOU WILL NEED

PTFE tape

Most washing machines and dishwashers are a standard size and have flexible hoses that make fitting very easy. Machines are supplied with PVC hoses that have a special valve to link to the water inlet. These valves allow you to turn off the water to the machine and service it or move it to a new place without having to call in a plumber, and without having to affect the water in the rest of the property.

Before you start, read the manufacturer's instructions. A brand-new washing machine will arrive with transit bolts fitted to the back of the machine. These must be removed before installation otherwise it won't work properly.

A new machine will come with two inlet hoses, blue for cold and red for hot. These connect to the back of the machine and can be screwed on. The other end connects to the water supply – note that the rubber ends connect to the water pipes and the filter ends connect to the machine. Some machines may only have a cold supply hose as the water is heated in the machine. In this case the fitting is exactly the same – you just need one less hose! Connect the hose/hoses supplied to the back of the machine and the other ends to the coordinating valves of the water supply. These connect by screwing together.

Plug in the machine to the power supply. Turn on the water valves connected to the copper pipes. Check for any drips and leaks. If there are any, turn the valves off and wrap some PTFE tap around the threads and then reconnect the valves. Turn the water on again, check again for drips and leaks.

The waste hose at the back of the machine normally just slots into a stand pipe or connects to a waste pipe loosely. Scoot the machine back into place and level the machine by adjusting its feet. Follow the makers' instructions for testing the machine and water pressure then wash your first load!!

Fixing a blocked toilet

DIFFICULTY RATING

YOU WILL NEED

Plunger
Snake (auger)

If you flush the toilet and the water rises to the rim, then you have a blockage in the trap or the drain. Don't panic. You can clear this fairly easily by using a plunger or a snake (also known as an auger).

To use the plunger, fit the rubber end snugly over the toilet waste pipe in the bowl and push up and down swiftly to invert the plunger head. This will cause air to be pushed and pulled in and out of the waste pipe creating a vacuum that should be enough force to push the blockage through. If this clears and the water starts to drain, flush the toilet a few times to really push the blockage out past the waste pipe.

If this doesn't clear the blockage then you may need to use a snake that winds down the toilet waste pipe and pushes against the blockage to break it up and move it along.

A long piece of stiff wire such as an old uncurled coat hanger can work if you don't have a plunger or an auger available – particularly handy if you are staying at some one's house and this happens! Not that I'm suggesting you should go around with a coat hanger in your bag 'just in case'. However, the best way to solve this problem is through taking preventive measures! Don't put anything down the toilet that you think might be difficult to flush, and then you shouldn't get this nasty problem.

Fixing a wonky toilet seat

DIFFICULTY RATING

If you have a wonky toilet seat or one whose lid won't stay up, you can try to make simple adjustments before deciding that a new seat is needed. The seat is bolted onto the toilet with a screw and washer. If you place your hand under the toilet at the back of the pan you should be able to feel these washers.

The screws are usually covered with little plastic covers. Lift these up and tighten or adjust depending on your problem. If this doesn't fix the problem, remove the screws and buy a new seat. They are easy to install especially if you have managed to remove the old one – you'll now know how it works!

Resealing a bath

YOU WILL NEED

Utility knife
Pliers
Washing-up liquid
White spirit
Kitchen towel
Cartridge gun
Silicone sealant
Disposable container
Old toothbrush

If you are starting to get black marks on the silicone sealant around your bath, this is a sign that mould is beginning to grow under it, which means that it is no longer water-tight. Your sealant could also start cracking and splitting, which will lead to water seeping in and causing damage to the wall behind the bath.

If you leave it too long, the gaps can get wider and water can pool on the floor beneath the bath. At best, it may cause a bad smell, at worst it will discolour the ceiling below if you have one and add another job to your to-do list. Better to do something about it.

Removing the old silicone

Cut a section of the old sealant with the knife and then use it to prise out a section large enough for you to get a grip on it. Holding on to the length of sealant, pull as much of the silicone out as you can. This can take a bit of effort but it's very satisfying! When a section breaks off, repeat until you have all the silicone out. Any extra bits that cling to the walls can be removed by gently cutting it away with the utility knife. There are silicone remover gadgets on the market that help as well.

Clean the area with white spirit to get rid of any residual silicone and any dirt. Pour 5 cm (2 inches) white spirit into a paper cup and use an old toothbrush to scrub the area covered by the silicone.

If there is a lot of black mould then use mould and mildew remover or bleach to kill off the mould and clean it out. If you don't clean it out thoroughly, the mould will just grow back under the silicone. Preparation is all...cleaning the surface well will pay off as it will be a longer time until you have to do it again. Once the area is clean and dry you can apply a new bead of silicone – it's best to buy one that is mould-resistant. Also make sure you buy the right colour, it's usually either white or clear but you can buy lots of different colours.

Using sealant

Cut the nozzle of the sealant tube as per the instructions. Don't cut a large section off as this will make for a large bead of silicone, which will be hard to work with. Fill the bath with water so that the bath is at its heaviest while you apply the silicone. If you don't do this, the next time you have a bath it will move away from the wall and the silicone will move, forcing it to crack and split.

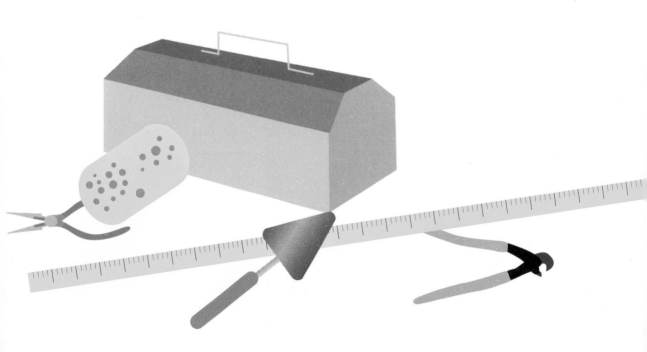

Running a bead of silicone around the bath

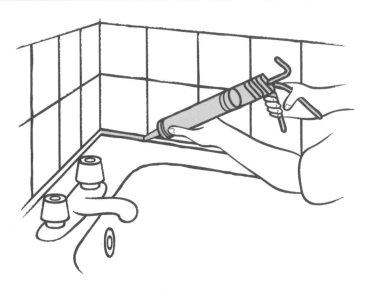

Silicone sealant and a cartridge gun are a menace in the wrong hands. Practise your silicone bead technique on a cardboard box before you allow yourself the pleasure of resealing your bath. Use even pressure and a steady hand to guarantee an even bead around the rim of the bath, enough to connect tile with bath.

Before you start using the silicone on the bath practise with a cardboard angle made from a cut-down cereal box so you get used to the force needed on the cartridge gun. Once you are happy with your squirting technique, start running a small bead of silicone around the edge of the bath. When you get to the end of the bath, release the pressure on the gun to stop the silicone flowing out.

Perfecting the finish

It is important to ensure that the sealant is well joined to the wall and the bath. Sealant is extremely sticky and there is a knack to not making a mess of your beautiful job at this point. There are several gadgets on the market that can smooth out any bumps you have made while running the sealant around the bath. However, you have a marvelous tool at your fingertips – it's your fingertip! Cover your finger with washing-up liquid and then run it along the middle of the silicone bead you have just created. You need to ensure that the bead spreads enough to join the wall and the side of the bath. When you get a build-up of silicone on your finger, wipe this off with a piece of kitchen towel and then repeat the process until you have created a nice neat seal between the wall and the bath.

Leave the silicone to dry with the water still in the bath, for at least 12 hours or longer, depending on the instructions for the product you've purchased. Once dry, clean off the excess washing-up liquid with warm water – oh, and you can let the water out of the bath now!

FLOORED – WHAT'S GOING ON UNDER YOUR FEET

When you are redecorating, how you treat the floors will have a tremendous impact on any room. You can carpet, paint, lay laminate flooring, vinyl or lino tiles. Your choice will depend on needs, desires and good old budget. By reading through how to deal with the different alternatives you can choose the solutions that are right for you.

If you have already decided that fitted carpet is the way for you, then get some prices for fitting from the store where you buy your carpet. Fitting carpet is a specialized job with some esoteric tools and requires quite a bit of brute force to get the stuff tight. The price you pay is probably worth it. A sagging carpet is very annoying.

What flooring

The simplest solution is to **paint** the bare surface. Bare floorboards or concrete flooring can be painted with floor paint, which is more robust than emulsion. There is no going back once it's done though; you can sand away the paint but this is a tough job. The next easiest solution is to lay **tiles**; you don't have to move out and they don't make too much mess. IF you do tile, lay the floor in sections and wait until the adhesive is dry before plonking all your furniture back on it.

Lino flooring – a little-known fact about linoleum is that it's an all-natural product and designs have come on in leaps and bounds since the days that it was fitted in your gran's kitchen. **Marmoleum®** is made from chalk, linseed oil and natural resins. It's SO durable it's probably in your local town hall corridors, but the new colours and ranges are breathtaking in their boldness.

Vinyl tiles are fabulously versi 'tile', inexpensive and really easy to lay. You could choose the classic black and white chessboard pattern for a retro look or use any of the hundreds of designs. The heavier

How much flooring?

To calculate how much flooring you require, measure the length of the room by the width and multiply to get the square meterage/yardage. Always add 10 per cent to allow for wastage, cuts, matching patterns, etc. Once you know the area you need to cover, you can get an idea of how much your various options will cost.

or more expensive the tile, the less likely it will be to rise because of thinner glue. If you do decide to use an inexpensive option, consider using additional 'grab adhesive' to keep it in place, especially if they are in the bathroom.

Laying vinyl tiles

YOU WILL NEED

Tape measure
Utility knife
Knee pads
Vinyl tiles
Adhesive and spreader

All surfaces to be tiled need to be sound, dry and flat, and when tiling floors the surface also needs to be level. It's a good idea to draw a scale plan of your floor to work out your pattern (if using one). You then need to find the centre of the room which is where you should start.

Vinyl tiles are easy to cut with a utility knife. Always use a straight edge and a sharp blade when doing this. Adhesive is applied to the floor using a spreader, then the tile is laid on top of it. Spread more adhesive and lay the next tile, taking care to butt-joint closely to the first tile. Remove any excess adhesive as you go along with a damp cloth (see cutting tiles pages 89 for further advice and instructions on cutting etc).

Vinyl on a roll is an inexpensive flooring solution as well. However, you will have to remove nearly everything from the room in order to fit it. If you are discarding an old vinyl floor, save the old floor to use as a template. If there are inaccuracies in the old floor, fill in the gaps on the pattern with tape so that the new one fits wonderfully.

Sanding and varnishing wooden floors

YOU WILL NEED

Sanding machines from a hire shop
Sanding belts
Goggles
Respiratory mask
Nail punch
Hammer
Interior wood varnish
Varnish brush
Knee pads

If you love the wooden floorboards you have found under the carpet then show them off! However, be aware that this is the Marine Corps end of this DIY book. This is where it gets really quite tough. Sanding your floor can sound like a daunting prospect, but these days many of us have moved away from carpets, and for allergy sufferers a bare floor provides fewer hiding places for the mighty mites.

There's plenty of clip-together wooden flooring available but if you've got real wooden floorboards you'd be mad not to put them on show. It's really not that complicated to sand a floor and it can completely transform a room.

Two things you should know before you decide to embark on sanding your wooden floors. Firstly, this is an incredibly messy job; it's extremely dusty and it's best done when the property is empty. If that's not a possibility then remove as much furniture as possible as you will need a clear floor; bear in mind your walls will get very dusty as well. So if you are thinking of decorating walls... decorate first. It's easier to remove dust than paint from a finished floor.

Secondly, if you want to do this work yourself it can be quite strenuous as the equipment is heavy. Make sure you can control the equipment properly. Go to a hire company and look at the sanding machines. Imagine pushing a really big vacuum cleaner through mud.

If you don't like the sound of either of these elements of the job, then you're better off getting a professional in to complete the work for you. There are lots of companies that will do this but ensure you get some recommendations and view pictures of previous work.

Preparation

To complete the task yourself you'll need to inspect the condition of the floorboards. If there are any nails sticking up tap them down with a nail punch and a hammer or remove and replace them; if left exposed they will rip the sanding belt. Look for patches of tiny holes that could be woodworm and treat any affected areas with chemicals and replace any boards that are deeply affected. You can take replacement boards from other areas of the house or purchase them from a reclaimed timber yard – check the dimensions since there is a variety of standard sizes depending on the period of the house.

Hiring equipment

You will need to hire both a drum flooring sander and an edging sander. Most hire companies will provide a sanding pack with all the equipment you need to complete a standard room, including three grades of sandpaper (coarse, medium and fine). If your boards are in very good condition, medium and fine will do.

Sanding

Block doors to other rooms with a drop cloth and open the windows if possible. Start in the furthest corner of the room with the drum sander and work your way systematically through the room with the medium grade sanding belt. Then apply the fine grade and work across the room following the length and grain of the boards.

To finish the areas near the skirting boards and in tight spaces you will need to use the edging sander. This allows you to get to those areas the drum sander can't reach. Once you have finished the main part of the floor, use the edging sander to blend in from the sanded area to the edges. When you are finished sanding, vacuum the floor then wipe with a damp cloth to remove all the dust.

It's a good idea to leave the room for a day before varnishing to allow all the dust in the air to settle. This will reduce the risk of dust settling on the wet varnish. Vacuum the floors again. You'll want to give your walls a good wipe too.

Varnishing

Consider filling the gaps in the floorboards before you begin to varnish (see the section on draught-proofing page 55). Work from the furthest point from the door. Wear knee pads. If you are staining the floor before varnishing, test colours on spare pieces of board similar to the floor itself and wet the sample to show its colour after the varnish coat dries. See how the colour looks in different parts of the room and at different times of day. What looks striking during the day may look gloomy at night.

There are a number of different varnishes on the market. Many traditional varnishes will have a high odour and need full ventilation, so wear a respiratory mask with replacable cartridges while using and open all the windows. Think about the other people and pets in the house if you are considering this method.

Modern methods of varnish production have increased the choices of non-toxic and low-odour products that are very durable. If you have small children and fish, these might be preferable. Once you've found one you like, apply with a good brush, following the grain. You will need two coats for depth and durability; allow each coat to dry completely. Make sure you paint your way out of the room and don't walk on the floor with shoes for at least two days! You wouldn't do the washing-up after painting your nails, so don't disturb the room until the varnish is completely dry.

Fixing a sticking door

DIFFICULTY RATING

YOU WILL NEED

Screwdriver
Sandpaper block
Sandpaper
Filler knife
Smoothing plane
Wood file
Stepladder

The problem of sticking doors can easily arise if you have installed a new floor surface and have consequently slightly raised the level of the floor. If you have a door that sticks so it doesn't shut properly, you can fix this fairly easily. If it isn't obvious where the door doesn't fit, be a detective. Take a look at the edge of the door to see if there are any telltale scuff marks to show where the door is rubbing. You can also run a knife blade around the closed door to find the sticking point. The knife will stop at the point where the door sticks. Shut the door as much as you can and with one eye closed, carefully see what areas of the door frame let light through.

If the door is painted, it may be that there is a build-up of paint causing it to stick. Remove the paint by sanding down the affected area. If this doesn't fix the sticking point then you will need to use a plane to shave the area. The plane will allow you to remove very thin strips from affected areas. If you don't have a plane, you can use a wood file or a rasp. If

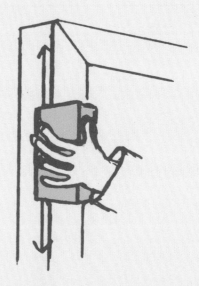

Use coarse sand paper to solve the problem of a sticky door.

the problem is at the side or the top of the door, then you can usually do this in situ by wedging the door open while you work. If the problem is at the bottom of the door, then you will need to remove the door from the frame (making this a slightly more challenging project).

When you remove the door, work the screws off by moving from top hinge to bottom. If you remove one hinge completely before you have even started on the next hinge, it makes the door very difficult to hold in place. Remove the screws from the frame side of the door so that the hinge is left on the door; this makes it much easier to refit once you've completed your task.

Lay the door somewhere flat, preferably on a work bench. A table covered with a drop cloth will also work but not the floor unless you have a way to raise the part you need to shave off. If the bottom is sticking because you have laid a new floor surface, you may need to trim the door using a jigsaw.

ON THE SHELF

Got too much storage? Didn't think so. We want it all, but where will we put it? Installing simple shelving need not be a difficult task and adds oodles of pleasure as all that stuff gets picked up off the floor and placed on the new surface.

The simple truth about floating shelves

Let's face the facts about these. **Floating shelves** may look like the perfect answer as they seem to hang without support and the photo on the pack is of a stylish interior, but take a long look at what is displayed on these shelves. A photo frame. A small vase with a flower. One more feather and the whole thing tumbles to the floor. These shelves are

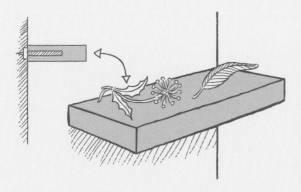

constructed of a hollow box with two holes on one length to fit over a metal frame that is anchored on the wall. A maximum of six screws hold the metal frame and so the loadage is going to be proportionate to the length and size of the screws and how secure they are fixed into the wall. The shelves cannot be cut to size as this will weaken the box. Yes, they look great, but if you are looking to load them up with books, think again. Feathers maybe!

Wire suspension shelves

A simple solution is to use a **wired suspension system.** The bracket is the wire that holds the

shelf. This requires a wall that can be drilled into, but unlike a floating shelf, the forces that hold the shelf have additional strength because they are directed back into the wall.

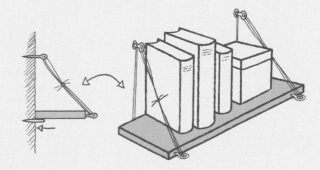

Alcove shelves

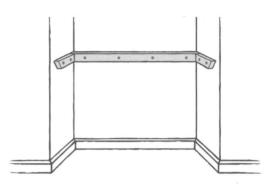

Fit battens to sides and back of alcove to support shelves.

The simplest shelves to make are those that fit in a recess or inside an existing cupboard, where the end walls are already in place. The sides of the recess or cupboard provide a surface to attach battens, which in turn support the shelving. Shelves can also be fitted between two cupboards to extend storage.

YOU WILL NEED

Lengths of batten
Jigsaw
Screws
Drill and bits
Tape measure
Spirit level
Clear varnish or paint
Paintbrush
Wood or melamine board for shelf

If the shelf required is small and the items are light, a simple solution is to fit battens on the left and right side walls of the alcove to support a free-sitting shelf fitted on top. Cut the battens slightly shorter than the depth of the shelf and maybe cut at an angle to rebate the batten. If the shelf is to carry heavy objects, place a batten on the back wall as well for extra strength (see 'Fitting a batten' page 48). The batten CAN be fixed to the front of a shelf instead of, or as well as a back wall batten. This look creates a boxy appearance and when sanded and painted, lots of novel effects can be achieved.

Fixing a bracket to a wall

If you need a shelf where there is no supporting side walls, then plan to use brackets, available from hardware stores or from lots of homeware shops if you are after a decorative look. Consider the length and weight of the shelves and plan to use enough brackets to bear the load and avoid sagging shelves later.

Use a spirit level to draw where the bottom line of the shelf will be. This will mark where the top of the bracket will be. Place brackets slightly in from the end of the shelves and position any additional brackets evenly. Use a bradawl to mark through the holes of the bracket to mark the position of the screws (see 'Fixing a screw into a wall', page 38).

WONKY FURNITURE – REPAIRING THOSE WOBBLES AND CREAKS

Before throwing out a less-than-perfect piece of furniture and replacing it with something new and expensive, use it to practise your budding DIY skills and renovate it to its former (cough cough!) glory. Even if it's made from chipboard and melamine veneer, making it well again will teach you skills you can use for more challenging projects. You will also be saving it from a sad and lonely fate in a landfill site. Kind to your wallet and kind to the planet!

Hanging hinges

DIFFICULTY RATING

Door hinges start to weaken, especially if there is a heavy mirror on the door. Take a look at the problem.

YOU WILL NEED

Slot and cross thread screwdrivers
Matchsticks
Glue
Two-part fast action wood filler

If the doors are held with modern kitchen-style hinges (see opposite) and they are overlapping or one door is higher than the other, then perhaps a simple adjustment with a manual screwdriver is all that is needed. Motor-driven screwdrivers are too enthusiastic and not subtle enough for the fine-tuning within the hinge so use a manual one. Decide which screws are holding well and which ones aren't working. Remove the door, loosening the screws from the bottom up. Get someone to help you if the door is heavy. If the screws have fallen out of the holes and the holes are now too big to hold them tightly, make the holes smaller by filling with fast-action wood filler or using matchsticks and glue. When the glue or filler has dried, replace the door and use a slightly larger (thicker, not longer) screw if possible, to hold the hinge in place.

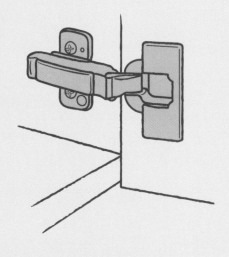

A kitchen-style hinge is easy to adjust

Wibbly wardrobe or bookcase

If you have a leaning tower of wardrobe or bookcase it is probably because the back has come away from the sides and needs to be repinned.

YOU WILL NEED

Small panel pins
Small hammer
Tape measure
Square
Rubber mallet
Nail set

If it's a big boy, clear a space to lay it down – get a friend to help you place it on its front. If the cabinet has kitchen-style hinges, you can remove them first to make it lighter (see previous page). On many flat-pack pieces of furniture, the back is made from a thin panel of hardboard and the small nails may have come away over time. Furniture is strained when it moves so this often happens after moving it from one place to another. Make sure the frame is square by measuring diagonally from the top left to bottom right and then top right to bottom left and adjusting the corners with a mallet after working out which way to nudge them with a square. They should all be the same measurement when finished. Sometimes the back panel will help to show which way the frame must be moved to make it square.

Consider using wood glue for extra welly. If you do, run a thin thread of glue in the groove when the frame has been made square. Place the first pin in the middle of one of the sides and the next pin in the middle of the opposite side. Do the same with the top and bottom. Now complete the pinning with pins placed evenly around the frame. If there IS a place where a screw could be hidden then use an extra screw to strengthen the back panel on the main body of the piece.

Wobbly wooden chair and droopy drawers

DIFFICULTY RATING

YOU WILL NEED

Ball of strong yarn/twine
Pencil
Wood glue
Fine sandpaper
Candle

Didn't your mum tell you not to lean back on chairs? She was right! Over time, the strain of leaning back on a chair will weaken the joints where the back leg meets the seat. The back of the chair suffers in the same way.

The thorough way of fixing this chair problem is to remove the wobbly legs and back, sand the glue gently from the joints and re-glue the whole thing. But if the legs are too stuck to pull out completely, there are several specialist expanding glues designed to fill the gaps while the joints are still together.

As clamping such an irregular shape is difficult using G-clamps or one-handed clamps, then a way to get everything to stay together is to use twine wrapped around the chair with a pencil or rod inserted and turned round to form a 'tourniquet'.

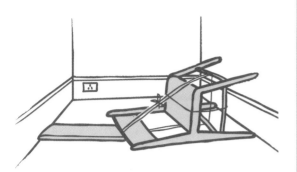

Holding the chair hostage while the glue dries.

Use soft clothes where the twine rubs the chair to avoid scratching the surface. Consider using a heavy object like a sofa to wedge the chair against a wall. Now, how you explain the trussed-up chair to an innocent visitor is entirely up to you.

Droopy drawers

Drawers are constantly under strain trying to keep our possessions in order and over time they may become weak and stiff. Fix the drawers one at a time, learning how they work as you go.

Remove the drawer. If it is on runners, there may be a fastening screw close to the front of the drawer. Loosening this will allow the drawer to lift out. Empty the drawer and turn it upside down. Check that all the screws holding the runners, if any, are tight.

Old wooden drawers run on wooden runners that wear and become dry. A traditional method of curing this problem is to take an old candle and rub it on the runners. The base of an old drawer should 'float within the frame'. Gluing them should be a last resort as the wooden drawer moves and the base may split.

Once all the drawers have been carefully removed and their positions noted, check that the metal runners (if it has these) still have all their screws in place. If it is a wooden carcass, rub the candle on the groove where the drawers run.

This whole operation can be very satisfying, combined a trip down memory lane as you retrieve long-lost socks and old love letters. And maybe while putting stuff back into the drawer you can do a bit of a cull and sort out what you really need – recycle the rest.

Knowing when to stop

Flaky veneers and stained wood surfaces may beg for something to be done but depending on your ability and the value of the object, it may be better to use the skills of a more experienced craftsperson. If you do work on a piece, use white wood glue as it is 'reversible' so that if more renovation is done at a later date, your work won't have permanently reduced the value. (More on reviving old furniture in 'Antique antics', see page 58.)

Pimp my closet – customizing an old wardrobe

DIFFICULTY RATING

Shoes running away from you? Buying things twice because you've forgotten the one lost in the mess? Can't find that belt? You need a closet makeover. Take a day off shopping for new things and spend it sorting out the stuff you've already got. You'll feel like you have a whole new wardrobe because you will have excavated everything you own. Careful thought and a few handy additions to the simplest closet can transform jumbled disorganization into a funky, functional dressing area.

YOU WILL NEED

Screwdriver set
Bradawl
Pencil
Level
Jigsaw
Melamine-coated particle boards
Small lengths of batten
Hooks
Mirrors
Mirror fixings/screws

Start with the doors

If you love those changing rooms with mirrors angled in all directions so you can see your gorgeous rear view, perhaps the doors of your closet can be used to recreate the same effect. Sometimes you can hang one mirror on a wall of the room and another on the outside or inside of a wardrobe door so that there is ample posing area in between.

Wall mirrors need special fixings, either corner fittings or special screws with domed screw tops. As mirrors are heavy, ask a friend to help you when you install it as it's quite a challenge to balance the screw

Fun House view

A word about very cheap mirrors. If the glass is very thin, the image will distort and you will be standing in front of a House of Fun (or Horrors) version of yourself. Place the mirror at an angle on the floor and walk back to take a peek at yourself. Look particularly at anything with a straight edge to make sure the image is true.

and the mirror at the same time. Not only will breaking a mirror bring seven years' bad luck, it can also result in a lot of clearing up and some very bad language indeed!

Half shelves

Often, there is enough space above a shelf to put in another that is half as deep. This stops too many sweaters having to be piled on top of each other. Using white melamine particle board instead of wood will ensure that the resin from the wood will not stain clothes that are left on the shelf. This technique of installing an extra half-shelf works in the kitchen too. Use the same techniques for installing shelves to alcoves by inserting batten supports (see 'Alcove shelves' page 106 and also refer to 'Fixing a screw into a wall', page 38–42).

Shoe story

Shoes will be better behaved and come when they are called if kept in a rack. Add a simple shelf to your wardrobe, angled towards the front. Put a small baton on the front of the shelf to form a lip that will stop your shoes from sliding down. A length of particle board held with batons can be screwed onto a door or a wall and shoes can be kept off the floor. Racks can also be made entirely with batons.

Hooks galore

DIY stores sell a variety of hooks from simple white clothes hooks to ornate and classic styles. It's up to you if you want to make the inside of your closet razzmatazz or minimalist style. Hang a double hook to hold belts, while plenty of single hooks will hold strappy bags and silky scarves.

Clothes rail

YOU WILL NEED

Chrome rod 25 mm (1 inch) diameter
End caps for fitting pole to wardrobe walls
Centre rail for extra support
Bradawl
Screwdriver

If you hoard clothes, you may need a heavier clothes rail – an extra-strong rail will hold lots more. Make sure you leave enough of a gap between the shelf above, if you have one, to lift out a clothes hanger; 75 mm (3 inches) is normally enough. Check the location of the clothes rail by holding a clothes hanger against the wall of the closet. Place the rail so that there is a small clearance between the back of the hanger and the back of the closet.

WINNING THE SWEDISH WAR

It's a classic scenario and the example often given by many people when they define their DIY capabilities: 'I can't even build flat-pack furniture'. Assembling flat-pack furniture doesn't have to be that painful, and you don't need a design degree to get to grips with putting the bits together.

Do a bit of planning before you go flat-pack shopping at the warehouse or via a catalogue. If you are ordering online and the flat-pack is being delivered, think about access to your building.

I recently wandered past a forlorn group in the street consisting of a disappointed woman and two frustrated delivery men trying to persuade a very large sofa into an apartment building.

Measure the doorway and space into which your desired item is going to fit. Don't build the bed in the living room and expect to carry it into the correct room because it might not fit through the door. If you are building tall units that are put together on their backs, make sure you have enough clearance space to stand them up.

...And becoming the flat-pack queen

DIFFICULTY RATING

YOU WILL NEED

Flat-pack of your choice
Cordless screwdriver and hex bit
Screwdriver bits
Tape measure
Mallet
Hammer
Wood glue
Combi square

Time-frame: longer than you might think. Don't berate yourself because it's not done in five minutes. The reason we pay less for receiving furniture in a flat-pack is because we aren't having to pay for the air inside the item when it's shipped and the company isn't paying for professionals to assemble it.

If you can, get someone to help you; it will make for a more efficient job as two pairs of hands ease the frustration of trying to hold something up and screw the joint in at the same time. Clear as much space as you can wherever you have decided to build the furniture. Remove anything precious that could be knocked over.

Preparation

Open the box and extract the instructions and diagrams and any clear plastic packs containing teeny tiny bits. Make a soothing non-alcoholic drink, then sit and try to absorb the instructions. The time spent with eyes glazed over incomprehensible words and microscopic diagrams will pay off later. Look out for phrases that begin 'DO

Sorting out the bits and pieces

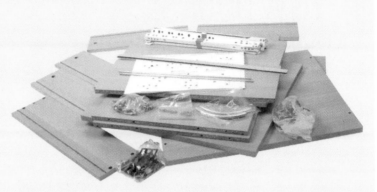

Find an empty egg box or roasting pan and tip the contents of the plastic packs into this container. It will deter the teeny tiny bits from escaping under the sofa. Sort out all the different bits, making lines and groups of all the different screws, dowel pegs, bolts and separate bits you don't recognize. Hold a roll call. Counting them and matching them up to the picture in the instructions will help you become familiar with them. The most common problem when building flat-packs is using the wrong screw and running out of the parts you need.

NOT REMOVE' or 'DO NOT GLUE...' Seeing, believing and hoisting these instructions on board will help make the construction process run much more smoothly and will prevent the onset of a great deal of unlady-like language.

Follow the diagram AND the instructions

A wild and wacky idea, I know, but it really is the key to success when waging the Swedish war. Use the picture as a guide for which way a panel has to go. Look carefully at the layout of the holes, for example, and match up with the real panel. Some diagrams are known as 'exploded isometrics'. They have illustrated how everything would 'un' fit together. Try the same thing yourself. Lay all the panels where they are in the diagram and work out what screw goes where.

Use a hex bit in a cordless screwdriver instead of the Allen key if possible. It saves time and doesn't make your hands so sore.

As you build the furniture, don't tighten the screws completely until all the pieces are in place.

Use a combi square to check that everything is at right angles and make the approriate adjustments.

Once all the parts are together, go round and tighten everything REALLY TIGHT. If the furniture fits together with wooden dowels, think about gluing these in place; certainly if you had bought a solid piece of ready-made furniture, it would be glued together. Drawers, in particular, take a lot of strain from the amount of stuff we expect them to hide (see 'Droopy drawers' page 111, for what happens when we overload these useful storage places).

Maintenance

If you haven't glued the piece of furniture together, it helps make it last longer if you occasionally retighten the screws and bolts.

KITCHEN REVAMPS – NEW DOORS, NEW SURFACES

If your kitchen is looking a bit shabby and worn at the edges, you can give it a whole new look and feel in a few simple steps, assuming you are happy with the layout and the units are in pretty good shape. Below you will find several suggestions ranging from the very easy to the quite challenging – pick and chose the ones that suit you to give your kitchen a facelift.

Kitchen cosmetic surgery

DIFFICULTY RATING

YOU WILL NEED

Drill
Drill bits
Screwdriver and bits
Tape measure
Jigsaw
Spirit level

Change the handles on the units

This one is dead easy. You can make a real impact really quickly. Handles can be changed easily but remember you will have holes where the current handles are, so make sure your new handles fit these holes. If your old handles are single knobs, you will find a large selection of choices and you have the option of drilling a second hole for a bar-type handle. If your existing handles have two holes, measure the distance from each hole and select from handles that have the same measurements.

Paint the door fronts

This is a slightly longer and more involved process, but painting the doors will make a big difference to your kitchen décor. Clean all the doors with sugar soap to remove all traces of grease and sand lightly to provide a key for the new paint. Use a hard enamel finish for a hard-wearing surface. You might find it easier to remove the doors from the units before you begin sanding and painting (see 'Hanging hinges' page 108 and also refer to preparation sections in 'Decor decorum', pages 62–83). This will allow you to move quickly from one door to the next.

Change the doors

If you are feeling a little more flush with money you might consider replacing the unit doors. There are many online companies selling brand-new

Soft closing doors

The luxury of modern kitchens is symbolized by smug, silent, soft-closing doors. By fitting damper mechanisms to the insides of your kitchen doors, you can enjoy the silence in your own kitchen. You will find packs of these in the kitchen section of large DIY stores – they are easily fitted with screws to the underside of your shelves.

doors for kitchen units, and most will show you what measurements you need. Some companies send a person around who will do all the measuring for you but these tend to be a little more expensive. If you are happy to go it alone, the first thing to do is measure your old doors carefully. If you are lucky and your doors are fairly new but maybe not to your taste, your units will be the same standard size as units sold in large DIY stores.

If your doors don't match any of the standard sizes widely available, try to find a company that will also cut the hinge holes for you, then fitting the new doors will be a breeze. If you measure the position of the hinge holes on your existing cupboards, the company can drill the holes in the appropriate position in your new doors.

If you change the unit doors, you can either re-use the hinges or buy new adjustable hinges. Don't despair if the door doesn't fit perfectly when you hang it; the hinges will take some adjusting for the door to fit properly. Use a hand screwdriver and slow-turn each adjustable screw of the hinge until the door fits well.

Revamp the splash-back

Retiling the splash-back is a great way to refresh the look of your kitchen especially if you choose some really funky, bright ceramic or glass tiles. (See 'On the tiles', page 85 for more information on tiling.) If you can't face the upheaval of removing the old tiles, then consider painting over the existing tiles in a new zingy colour. Make sure the old tiles are completely free of grease by washing with sugar soap and scrubbing them until they are squeaky clean. Thoroughly rinse off the sugar soap. Use gloss paint so that the new surface can be wiped down and cleaned easily.

Another method of revamping the splash-back is to use Amtico® tiles instead of ceramic ones. Like vinyl tiles, they don't have to be grouted and so will have a seamless finish. Ensure that the splash-back area is thoroughly cleaned with sugar soap before you begin and use a high-impact adhesive to hold the tiles. Don't use this method near the stove or hob as the tiles may get too warm and melt!

Change the hob splash back

Add a new look by changing the splash-back behind the hob. Replace stainless steel by unscrewing the panel and install brightly coloured tempered glass. These panels are made in several different sizes and are treated to withstand high temperatures.

THE GREAT OUTDOORS

If you are lucky enough to have some outdoor space then you will want it to be as pretty and practical as possible. That means taking care of outdoor furniture and adding a few DIY embellishments – hanging baskets, solar lights, maybe even an artificial lawn!

Hanging things to exterior walls

DIFFICULTY RATING

YOU WILL NEED

Drill
Masonry drill bits or wooden ones depending on wall
Bradawl
Chalk/marker pen
Masking tape
Goggles
Wall fitting/screws
Brackets etc
Masonry/wood paint
Brushes

We have talked through the basics of drilling into walls and how to hang things to interior walls (see fixing things to walls, pages 38–41). Well, outside is no different. You will need to use masonry drill bits on masonry walls (brick) and wood bits on wooden areas such as decking and fencing. Simple objects such as a door number or a 'Beware of the Cat' sign will only require 25 mm (1 inch) or smaller screws. If you ARE putting a number on your house, consider the viewpoint of someone in a car. Bigger numbers or clear markings on a gate will make your delivery person a happy chappy.

If you want to put up something like a hanging basket you will need to mark the wall where you want the basket to go, bearing in mind that if it's too high you won't be able to water it. Ask someone to hold it in place for you to make sure you like where it is before you start fixing it to the wall. Mark the wall with something visible such as a black marker pen or chalk (pencil really isn't going to show up on brickwork). You can even apply some masking tape to the area and then mark your hole on that.

Use a bradawl to create a tiny hole for the drill bit to grip into and start making your hole with the appropriate-sized drill bit. If you are struggling to make a hole to start with, then try a smaller pilot hole before going for a bigger drill bit. Drilling into

🔧 Trade secret

Use galvanized or coated screws to stop them from rusting. If the screws rust they become brittle and weak, can break easily, and also look really nasty!

masonry is quite hard work and can take a bit of effort and power so make sure your drill is in hammer mode if it has that setting. Needless to say, you should be wearing your protective goggles!

Fit the chosen wall fixing into the hole you have made and then screw in the hanging basket bracket. Make sure it is secure as you will be adding additional weight every time you water the plants.

Use the same method for hanging anything – from

an outdoor canopy to external lights. With lighter items, you might just get away with nailing them into place, especially if you are only planning to leave these items outside during the summer months – light fairy lights and lanterns spring to mind.

Lighting

Exterior lighting means that you can use your garden any time of the day or night, weather permitting. For lights that are wired in you will need to get an electrician to put in the appropriate external wiring, but there is plenty of solar-powered lighting on the market that is easy to fit. Being solar powered means that energy is stored during the day to be used at night; don't worry – it doesn't require brilliant sunshine for it to work.

Most of these lights can be fitted to the wall using the steps outlined above for fixing things to walls. These are great for security and you can buy ones with sensors so that they light up if there are any intruders in the garden (although they do light up when cats and foxes creep across the grass in the middle of the night too!). Consider it a free floor show and be glad the lights are working.

Bringing colour into the garden

Not everyone has green fingers, but you can bring colour into your garden without touching a trowel! Paint for wooden fences now comes in a vast array of shades, which means you can add a splash of colour and cover those boring shades of green and brown. Painting a wooden fence doesn't just make it look good, it protects the wood from weathering so it's vital to do this every few years.

If you have brick walls in your garden you can also paint these funky colours – shop online for interesting colour masonry paints. You can't use normal emulsion as it won't be sturdy enough to weather the winter. The ranges of masonry paints are still less vibrant than indoor emulsions, but with a bit of imagination and research you'll be able to find something of interest.

Consider some outdoor artwork; create your own with some help from a spray can (you know you've

always wanted to give those graffiti artists a run for their money). You can also put up outdoor mirrors (usually made of robust plastic) to increase the feeling of space. If you choose a glass mirror, make sure you are comfortable with it tarnishing and pitting over time. Secure it safely with 'grab it' adhesive or brackets so that your serenity isn't interrupted with a smashing bit of bad luck.

 Trade Secret

When you paint be aware of seepage through to the neighbour's fence! There are a number of flashy gizmos on the market that claim you can spray-paint your fence in super quick time, however, these can cause a lot of paint to fly through the cracks in your fence into your neighbour's garden. So if you don't want to spray-paint their roses a dark brown then you are best off sticking with a brush. It's good for the bingo wings (if a little tedious).

Fitting a water butt

DIFFICULTY RATING

YOU WILL NEED

Masking tape
Hacksaw
Water butt and water butt kit
Diverter (if not included in your kit)
Drill

If you want to make your garden a bit more environmentally friendly there is one simple thing you can do – fit a water butt to collect rain water. It's usually made of soft moulded plastic and can be purchased from most decent hardware stores or online retailers. It can be fitted to your drainpipe and collects the rain water that drains off the roof. You can then use the water to clean your car or water the plants, both saving on water bills and saving the planet.

Water butts usually stand on the floor but smaller

1. Position butt near pipe, then measure line on pipe level with top of butt. Cut out section where marked.

2. Fit hose-fitting section to the down pipe and seal with PTFE if necessary.

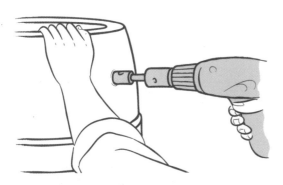

3. Drill hole in butt the same size as the hose connector.

4. Fit flexible hose to connectors.

The second method involves cutting a small hole in the drain pipe and installing a rain water diverter (see illustrations on page 125). You will need to use a hacksaw or a wall board saw to cut the hole out of the drain pipe. To make this easier, drill a couple of small holes (being careful not to drill through to the other side of the drain pipe) along the line you need to cut; this acts as a guide and also makes it less tiring on your arm muscles.

Locate a suitable downpipe with plenty of space around it for the water butt. Place the water butt on its stand in front of the downpipe and mark the height on the downpipe. Use a hacksaw to cut the downpipe about 3 cm (1¼ inch) below this mark and fit the rainwater diverter here. Attach the rain water diverter to the water butt with the supplied fittings and ensure the water butt is secure on its stand. If it looks like it may wobble when full then attach to the wall using a bracket.

Fit the rainwater diverter to the cut-out section of the butt. When the water butt is full, the water will be diverted back to the drainpipe as originally designed. Remember when fitting your water butt that the tap should be facing forwards and there should be enough room for you to fit a watering can or bucket underneath. If you have a large water butt you need to make sure it is sitting level on the floor, otherwise it may topple over when full (possibly taking the drain pipe with it) so sit it on a paving slab, or attach it to the wall with brackets.

ones can be fixed to the wall if you are limited on space. If you want to connect a water butt to your down pipes you will need to ensure that your pipes are plastic and not old-fashioned lead ones that are much harder to cut into and not recommended at all. Depending on the water butt fitting kit you have bought, your butt should have a rain water diverter with it. If it doesn't you can purchase this separately.

Installation

There are two main methods for installing a water butt. The first involves removing the bottom section of the drain pipe and fitting the butt underneath so that the water collects directly into the butt (see photo above for this attachment). Make sure the water butt has an overflow pipe directed into the drain so that when the butt is full, the water can drain away as designed (rather then flooding your garden).

Faking it – artificial lawn

DIFFICULTY RATING

YOU WILL NEED

Lengths of artificial lawn
Utility knife
Sealant if you need to join lengths
Bag of fine sand

Ahh, the sound of the mower and the smell of new-mown grass. NOT!

If you live in a basement and your only outside space can't keep ivy alive, consider how sumptuous it would be to walk and laze on a soft grassy surface – enter the world of new types of artificial lawn. Small patches of real lawn can be tough to maintain in a shady and badly drained area; the sad tufts of grass that do make it through the moss, mud and weeds require cutting and necessitate storing or borrowing a lawn mower. Thousands of gallons of harmful chemicals get poured onto lawns to encourage them to perfection.

You can lay artificial grass on anything: concrete is transformed without having to go through sledge hammer hell. If you are laying it on bare earth, level out the ground with a long piece of plank and a rake. Take your time; it is going to be worth it in the end. Work out how much you need using the same criteria as laying carpet, vinyl tiles or wood flooring (see 'Floored' page 99).

Artificial grass has a grain, so if you are patching, be aware that the grass will look different from different angles. You will need an underlay – a weed barrier – and that is easily cut with a sharp utility knife. The artificial grass is joined together with green sealant. After installation, spread fine sand over the grass to fall into the mesh and hold it down.

To maintain artificial grass, you only need to sweep it with a hard broom. Don't get carried away with thinking it's real – stubbing out cigarettes will cause permanent damage and remember that if you choose to do DIY on your artificial lawn, you need to be careful not to paint it, singe it, or smother it with sawdust as it WON'T GROW BACK!

Maintaining outside furniture and woodwork

YOU WILL NEED

Preserving oil or varnish
Paint brush or pad
Solvent to clean up
Plastic or latex gloves
Plastic drop cloth
Plastic furniture studs for tables and chairs
Sandpaper

Maintaining outside furniture provides a good workout and is an excellent way to get rid of the winter blahs. Buy wood varnish in advance as the days grow longer and use the first warm morning to blow the cobwebs off your garden furniture and out of your head. Most purchased garden furniture will have been treated with a preserving oil during its manufacture, but to extend its life, you should really apply another coat before you actually put it outside.

Lay down a protective plastic dust sheet so that drips don't mark the ground surface. You can use old newspaper or cardboard but plastic is less likely to stick to the furniture as it dries. Wear plastic or latex gloves as you will need to handle the wet furniture as you move it around. Use either a brush or a pad to apply the wood preserver. Needless to say, read and follow the instructions on the tin!

Turn the chair, table or box upside down and paint the ends of the feet. The more preservative you can get into the end grain, the longer it can withstand sitting in the gloomy rain. To provide extra protection, knock in plastic furniture studs to lift the wood away from the wet ground. Treat all the surfaces you can get to while the object is upside down, working in a methodical manner from upturned feet down to the ground – this ensures that falling drips get wiped away.

Turn the object on its side and now work methodically painting each side, then turn it around. Finally, stand the chair, table or box up and treat the surface areas. Modern preservers are quick-drying and can be sanded in between coats.

Once dry, finish table tops and arms of chairs by scouring very lightly with steel wool.

If the furniture has to stay outside under snow and months of wetness, not even the most rigorous routine will win the battle of ageing. Help it last longer by putting it in the shed or swathing with plastic covers during the winter months.

If you choose not to maintain hardwood, it will develop a cool silver appearance and the grain will open slightly with the seasons and mellow. Small cracks are normal and won't effect the stability. Unpainted softwood will absorb moisture, rot eventually and one day may lose you some of your hard-won dignity when a chair breaks beneath you. Don't say you weren't warned!

Cat or dog flap

If Felix or Fido is testing your patience with attention-grabbing presents in the litter tray or performing the world famous 'Look at me, I want to be on the other side of the door' routine, then it's time to cut those apron strings and wake up to Independence day.

YOU WILL NEED

Cat or dog flap kit
Tape measure
Marking square
Pencil
Drill and bits
Jigsaw
Screws
Screwdriver
Mastic and gun

7 ⬛ *In a flap*

You might consider fitting a pet flap and collar combo that allows your Felix or Fido into the house, but keeps out all the other Toms, Dicks and Harrys. The collar acts as a key!

Decide where the flap will best suit cat or dog and staff (you) – it might be a panel in a back door. Ensure that the animal in question will be at the correct height to approach it from both sides. You may need to make a step with a couple of bricks outside if the ground is on a different level.

Cat flaps are made for different thicknesses of wood or glass so make sure you buy one that is suitable for the task. Read the instructions on the pack to find out the size of opening you will need to cut. To cut a hole in a wooden panel, measure and mark the rectangle needed and make a pilot hole with a drill. Increase the size of the hole so that it large enough to use a pad saw or insert the blade of a jigsaw. Screw the flap into the panel and enjoy the unbridled thanks from your cat, or not, as the case may be.

CHICKEN RUN/GARDEN CLOCHE

A simple wooden framework can be knocked together using basic screwing and joining techniques and adapted to a lot of different uses:

✔ Covered in chicken wire it will be a haven for your egg-laying fluffies. Wear gloves to cut the chicken wire as it is a bit aggressive in its springiness. Use a staple gun to hold the wire onto the frame or use staple nails and a hammer.

✔ To cosset cucumbers, cover the frame in polythene and let the sun shine in. Polythene can be cut with a utility knife. Use galvanized nails with wide heads to hammer and hold onto frame.

✔ A frame covered in chicken wire can also be a temporary protection system to protect fish ponds from unwanted visitors.

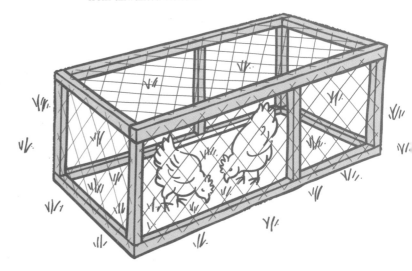

A simple frame can be made into a daytime chicken run or cold frame.

Glossary

One of the biggest complaints directed at tradespeople is their tendency to use overly complex technical language to try to justify the fee for the job they've been asked to do. Most people would prefer straightforward language so they can understand what they are getting and what they are paying for. So jargon busting...

Aggregate sand and or **stone chippings** added to cement to create concrete. Can also be mixed with paint to create a textured finish.

Air brick a brick with holes through it that allows air to circulate through a room. It can be installed at the bottom or top of a wall to alleviate condensation.

Airlock where air has caught in your plumbing pipes; can cause funny noises and inhibit the efficiency of radiators.

Architrave decorative wooden moulding that sits around doors and windows covering the gaps left between the frame and the wall.

Asbestos an out-moded material used for insulation. Very hazardous to health and must be removed by a specialist. If you suspect you have asbestos don't touch it.

Asphalt tar-like adhesive usually applied to flat roofs.

Auger mechanical tool used to bore holes. Drain augers can be used to unblock drains and toilets.

Baluster chunky post that supports a handrail on a staircase.

Balustrade safety barrier that runs along staircase or landing.

Bannister handrail that runs up a staircase.

Batten a piece of wood used to fix things into place.

Beading small convex wood moulding used to cover expansion gaps in floors or as general trim.

Blown plaster plaster that has become detached from the wall and turned to powder.

Breeze block various types of building blocks, usually made from cement.

Building regulations laws that outline what materials, building layouts and methods can be used in certain building work to ensure durability and safety.

Cavity wall continuous gap between inner and outer brickwork. Cavity wall insulation is where this gap is filled with foam or polystyrene beads to increase insulation.

Chase a channel cut out of masonry or brick to house electrical cable or pipework.

Chipboard material used for flat-pack furniture or kitchen units. Made of wood chips glued together in sheets and can be covered with melamine.

Circuit a complete wiring path through which electrical current flows.

Cistern tank for storing water.

Combi combination gas boiler that heats water instantly so you don't need water tanks and hot water cylinders. Space-saving and energy-efficient, also gives better water pressure than other types of boilers.

Combi drill a tool that is a combination of drill and hammer drill for harder surfaces.

Condensation occurs when warm air meets a cold surface, causing water drops on surfaces such as ceilings and windows. When this water forms on absorbent surfaces it can soak in and lead to mould. The solution is improved ventilation.

Consumer Unit used be to called a fuse board. This box takes the mains electricity into a property and distributes it to various circuits.

Coping/coping stone a decorative stone or concrete finish that sits on the top of a wall to prevent rainwater soaking into the wall.

Cornice/coving decorative moulding fitted at the top of a wall where it joins the ceiling.

CORGI see Gas Safe Register.

Countersink a hole that allows a bolt or screw to fit flush with the surface.

Dado rail decorative wooden moulding that sits around the lower part of an interior wall.

Damp proof course (DPC) a layer of waterproof material that stops water soaking into the brick of a building from the ground.

Door jamb vertical pieces of wood on each side of the door frame.

Dormer window a window placed in the slope of a roof.

Dry rot a fungus that attacks wood, causing it to crumble and become structurally unsound. Usually happens in moist environments.

Earth electrical connection to the ground to channel a reliable conductive path to the ground.

Eave overhang of the roof beyond the wall.

Elbow right-angle joint for pipework and ducting.

Edging strip/bead moulded wood or veneer trim over the edge of furniture to hide the chipboard and provide a tidy finish.

Epoxy synthetic resin that provides super-strong adhesive, very tough stuff!

Expansion gap space left when fitting wooden floors to allow for natural expansion and contraction of the wood.

Exterior paint durable paint with binder and pigments to ensure it can resist the elements.

Fascia strip of wood that covers the end of the rafters and where guttering is fixed.

Feather to gently wear away until an edge is covered, can be done with paint, sanding or delicate woodworking.

Fire door highly resistant door that often has a self-closing mechanism and provides an additional 30 minutes of protection in the case of a fire. It is a legal requirement to fit these as internal doors in flats to minimize the risk of fire spreading.

First fix when the pipework, electrical cables, carpentry is done before the plastering.

Flashing normally made from metal this material sits over roof joints to prevent leaks.

Flat roof a roof with only a very small gradient for drainage, essentially looks flat.

Flexible hose a hose made from interlocking metal that can be fitted in tight spaces where hard pipework is not possible. Usually found on taps and under baths.

Floor joist light beam that supports the floor.

Flue a duct to allow heat and gas to escape from a boiler or fireplace.

Flush door flat-faced door.

Formica high-pressure laminate that can be used for furniture, work surfaces.

French door exerior double doors, mainly glazed.

Fuse board see consumer unit.

Fuse spur a fused power outlet to which an electrical cable is connected directly without the need of a plug.

Gas Safe Register the official registration body for gas engineers in the UK (people that are legally qualified to work on gas plumbing). Used to be called CORGI registration. If you are having any gas work done it must be undertaken by a GSR plumber.

Gate valve a valve the stops the flow of water by an internal gate being lifted or dropped within the valve.

Galvanize to cover in a protective zinc layer.

Gang group of sockets (2 gang = double socket).

Grain the direction of the wood fibres within timbers.

Grout powder mixed with water to provide the material between tiles.

Guttering the pipework that filters rainwater from the roof to the drainage system.

Hacksaw lightweight metal cutting tool.

Hairline cracks very fine cracks that appear on the surface but do not penetrate.

Half-round moulding used for decorative finishes.

Hammer drill pneumatically powered mechanism within the drill that allows the drill to penetrate harder surfaces.

Header tank small tank that feeds water to the central heating system.

Hearth fire-resistant section on the floor in front of a fireplace.

Hipped roof a pitched roof where the sides are also sloped.

Hollow wall continuous gap between the inner and outer brick to allow for air circulation (usually a 50 mm/2 inch gap).

Impermeable material that does not allow the passage of liquid.

Inspection chamber a small space covered by a manhole cover to inspect drains and sewer systems.

In situ to work on something in its place rather then removing it and re-installing.

Insulation materials used to cover or protect from heat items such as electrical wires, cold water pipes or to reduce the transmission of heat and sound.

Inhibitor oxidant added to coatings and pipework to stop corrosion and other undesired effects.

Intake valve pipe or area where gas and water comes in to property.

Interior wall a wall that has no external face.

Isolation valve small valve on water pipes that allows water to be stopped to that appliance.

Jigsaw electric saw that allows free and easy cuts.

Joist timber beam used in ceiling, floor or roof construction.

Joiner Specialized craftsperson who makes cabinets and furniture.

Junction box a small box that allows electric cables to run off in different directions.

Key a scratch on the surface of paint to provide a rough area for the paint to adhere.

Knot hard cross-grain section on wood where a branch has met the trunk.

Knotting solution thin varnish to stabilize the weak point in the wood; this stops the knot from showing through paint work over time and can prevent it from warping the wood.

Lagging insulation around pipework and tanks to prevent frost.

Laminate type of wood covered with veneer; can be used for work surfaces or flooring.

Lath and plaster an old method of finishing a timber-framed wall or ceiling. Narrow strips of wood (laths) are nailed to the studs (wall) or joists (ceiling) to provide a supporting framework for plaster.

eco paint

Lean-to sloping structure that sits against the side of a wall; can be used as a conservatory or utility area.

Lintel structural wood, steel or brick section above a window to support the wall above the window opening.

Linoleum inexpensive floor covering made from cork and linseed oil, very natural and environmentally friendly.

Load-bearing wall a wall that supports the load from above; if you want to remove one of these you will need to install an RSJ (rolled steel joist) in its place.

Making good repairing an area of damage and providing the finishing touches.

Mantel shelf or trim above fireplace.

Marine ply exterior-grade plywood, can get wet.

Mastic waterproof silicone sealant used to seal joints.

Mark-up price that is added to materials or work to cover sourcing fees.

Membrane impervious layer of materials used in roofing, tanking.

Mezzanine an additional half-floor inserted between floor and ceiling (usually in high buildings).

Mist coat thin coat of paint used on newly plastered walls to prime the walls for paint (mix 10 percent water into emulsion paint).

Mitre a 45-degree cut or joint in wood.

Mortar sand and cement mix used in between bricks.

Mortise and tenon joint in wood that is very strong, the mortise is a hole cut into the wood and the tenon is the piece that goes into the mortise. Can be glued or screwed together.

Nail pointed metal with a head at the end for joining materials together.

Nail set/nail punch tapered steel rod that allows nails to be driven under the surface of the material.

Needle-nose pliers very thin pointed pliers for use in confined spaces.

Newel large post supporting the staircase handrail at the bottom of the stairs.

Nibblers tool used to snip small sections of tile away.

P-trap fitted under sinks and toilets to provide a water seal.

Panel door a door with panelled patterns in wood.

Panel pin very small thin nail to attach wood mouldings.

Parapet (wall) low wall along the edge of roof or balcony.

Parting bead strip of wood that sits between two sash windows.

Parquet flooring composed of small blocks of wood in geometric patterns.

Party wall a wall shared between neighbouring properties, where both parties have equal rights over the wall.

Pebble dash exterior render with stones/glass bits embedded in it for decorative effect.

Pendant central light fitting that drops from ceiling to which a shade can be fitted.

Pilot hole a small hole drilled before to give a screw guidance.

Pitch the angle at which a roof slopes.

Plane a tool used to skim small slivers of wood from a surface to make fine alternations such as when a door is sticking.

Plasterboard prefabricated boards used for interior wall and ceiling coverings.

Pliers pincer-like tool.

Plumb line cord with a weight (plumb bob) on the end to create a straight vertical line.

Pointing smooth outer edge of the mortar between bricks.

Prime first coat of paint that protects a surface and stops absorption from other coatings, usually a thinner layer of paint.

Profile the outline of an object.

PTFE plumbers' tape of polyurethane that helps seal threaded joints.

Public liability insurance insurance covering liability of the insured for negligent acts resulting in bodily injury or death, and property damage.

Rafter a sloping beam forming the structure of the roof.

Ratchet device that permits movement in one direction only.

Rake out action to remove debris from crack.

Rawl plug brand name of wall fixing.

Render a general wall covering, usually plaster but can be cement, pebble dash or stucco.

Repointing is needed when mortar between bricks crumbles and needs to be replaced.

Retaining wall a wall used to support earth or any pressure from the other side.

RCD (Residual Current Device) fuse that monitors the flow of electrical current through the live and neutral wires of a circuit. When an RCD detects an imbalance caused by earth leakage, it cuts off the supply of electricity as a safety measure. Normally fitted to high current devices such as electric showers and cookers.

Ring main power circuits for wall sockets.

Rising damp moisture absorbed from the ground causing damage to brick, wood, plaster and decoration. Normally a sign of a missing or damaged damp-proof course.

Rock wool coarse insulating material made from fibre glass.

Rout to cut a large groove or gap (usually with a router), for decoration or sealants etc.

RSJ (rolled steel joist) installed to support the load when a load bearing/supporting wall is removed.

Sash window usually wooden windows that slide parallel to each other.

Screed layer of fine concrete normally applied to walls for a flat finish.

Second fix finishing work done normally after the plastering; fitting and connecting sockets and switches, sinks, basins, doors etc.

Sanding block small piece of wood wrapped in sandpaper to allow for a better grip and a flatter surface when sanding.

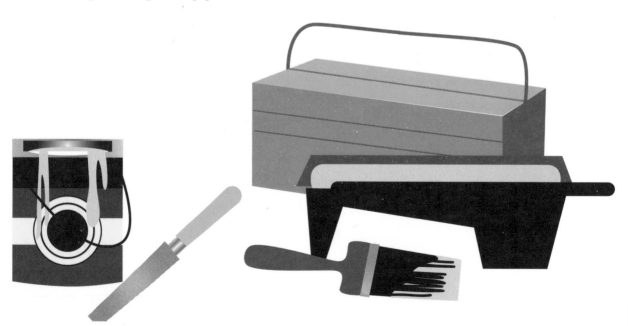

Short circuit where the current is accidentally re-routed and increases the flow thereby causing the fuse to blow.

Siphon mechanism with the toilet.

Skim top layer of finishing plaster.

Snagging once a project has been finished a snagging list notes all the areas where touch ups or further work needs to be done to complete the job.

Soil pipe vertical pipe that carries sewage directly from the building into the sewer.

Stack vertical pipes that carry waste from toilets and sinks to the soil pipe.

Staff bead innermost section of wood that holds a sash window in place.

Stud wall interior wall (not load-bearing) built from 2 x 4 timber frame and covered with plasterboard to divide two rooms.

Stop cock isolating tap valve that stops mains water from entering the property.

Subsidence where the soil has moved beneath or beside a property causing the property to move. Can be caused by water being taken from the soil by tree roots, or drainage systems flushing away the soil.

Tanking installing a membrane to ensure an area is waterproofed; for example, behind tiles or in basements.

Trap waste pipe under a sink that carries away the water.

TRV thermostatic radiator valve that allows you to adjust the temperature of one radiator.

Undercoat a layer of paint that provides a good seal for timber and better adhesion for the top coat.

Underlay soft spongy material used under carpets and flooring to create a flexible surface; can be made from rubber, foam or fibre board.

Underpinning normally needed due to subsidence, this method of construction involves providing support beneath a column or a wall, without removing the superstructure, in order to increase the load capacity or improve the original structure of the building.

Veneer thin decorative laminate covering over chip board.

Washer flat rubber/metal device to create a watertight seal in plumbing.

Warp twist in materials such as wood.

Wet rot damage and decay of timber as a consequence of water, this is less serious then dry rot but needs to be treated quickly.

Wet trades refers to plastering and rendering.

Wood filler specific filler for timber, this paste or liquid dries hard enough to fix things into it.

Index

Picture credits